TENNIS AND OXFORD

By the same author

HISTORY
Good King Richard? (1983, reprinted 1994)
Pretenders (1986, reprinted 1987)

Independent Television in Britain:
Vol. 3. Politics and Control, 1968–80 (1989)
Vol. 4. Companies and Programmes, 1968–80 (1990)

FICTION
Hazard Chase (1964, reprinted 1989)
The Primrose Hill Murder (1992)

JEREMY POTTER

Tennis and Oxford

FOREWORD BY THE RT HON.
LORD ABERDARE KBE

OXFORD UNICORN PRESS
1994

© 1994 The Unicorn Club
Published by Oxford Unicorn Press,
The Tennis Court, Merton Street,
Oxford OX1 4JD

All rights reserved. No part of
this publication may be reproduced,
stored in a retrieval system, or transmitted, in any form
or by any means, electronic, mechanical,
photocopying, recording or otherwise,
except as permitted by the UK Copyright,
Designs and Patents Act 1988,
without the prior permission of the copyright owner.

First published 1994

A catalogue record for this
title is available from the British Library

ISBN 0 9523197 0 5 (trade edition)
ISBN 0 9523197 5 6 (de luxe edition)

Printed in Great Britain at the Alden Press Ltd,
Oxford and Northampton
and bound by Hartnolls Ltd,
Bodmin, Cornwall

Contents

	List of Illustrations	vi
	Foreword *by The Rt Hon. Lord Aberdare KBE*	viii
1	An Intellectual and Unlawful Pastime	1
2	Origins and Growth	8
3	The Golden Age	18
4	Early Days in Oxford	28
5	College Ball Courts	33
6	Courts, Inns and Theatres	56
7	The Blue Boar Courts	63
8	The Oriel Street Courts	67
9	The First Merton Street Court	77
10	A Dynasty of Champions	82
11	The Nineteenth-Century Renaissance	89
12	Modern Times in Oxford	106
	Appendix A: Playing the Game	125
	Appendix B: Oxford Blues and Half-Blues 1947–1994	132
	Acknowledgments	136
	Source References	138
	Index	147

List of Illustrations

In the Text

Tennis Play	6
The Moat Court at Windsor Castle	14
A 19th-Century Racket	17
A 17th-Century Paris Court	20
The Future King James II on Court	26
Christ Church Ball Court	44
Ball Play in Merton College	47
Oriel College Ball Court	49
Pembroke College Ball Court (1675)	50
Pembroke College Ball Court (1700)	51
University College Ball Court	52
An Uncovered Ball	69
Letter from the Future King Edward VII	93
Putto at Play	123
Internal View of a Court	124

Plates

The Merton Street Court	*Frontispiece*

Tradesmen's Tokens
First Letter from Visitor of Brasenose
Second Letter from Visitor of Brasenose
Tuition of Prince of Wales on Oriel
    Street Court   *[Between pages 56 and 57]*

List of Illustrations

James Russell, Keeper of the Oriel Street Court
Edmund Tompkins the Fourth, World Champion
Tom Pettitt and George Lambert, World Champions
Thomas Stone
The Lords Aberdare
Chris Ronaldson, World Champion
Richard Montgomerie
1994 OU Women's Team with Coach

[*Between pages 104 and 105*]

Foreword
The Rt Hon. Lord Aberdare KBE
President of The Tennis and Rackets Association

IT IS remarkable that as time goes by and the past gets ever more remote, scholars in many fields discover more and more about it. This is very true of tennis, which has such an ancient tradition, and the Oxford University Tennis Club and The Unicorn Club are to be congratulated on marking the 400th anniversary of tennis in Merton Street with this publication.

Jeremy Potter has done a real service to the story of tennis at Oxford by his painstaking research into College, University and City records. His book will now become the standard work on the subject.

Oxford is one of the main sources of recruits to tennis, and I am sure that many present and future players will find additional interest in the game when they read of its past popularity in the University and City.

Jeremy Potter has achieved a remarkable double. He is already well-known as the author of *Hazard Chase*, a work of fiction first published in 1964. Now thirty years later, he has written a work of fact that is equally deserving of our admiration and thanks.

CHAPTER I

An Intellectual and Unlawful Pastime

TENNIS – real tennis – is the most intellectual as well as the most historic of ball games. Humanists in the sixteenth century recognised it as an ideal combination of physical and mental exercise. Philosophers have been eloquent in its praise. Parallels have often been drawn with chess. It is fitting therefore that Oxford should have played a significant role in the long history of this game. In the words of the Amateur Champion of the day writing in 1890 (with a pardonable measure of exaggeration): 'Almost every sapling that has grown into a forest tree in the microcosm of Tennis has been planted and watered in the nurseries of Oxford or Cambridge.'[1]

Galleries, sloping roofs, a drooping net and the other peculiarities of a strangely asymmetrical court, in which solid balls can be cut, twisted or spun at will, offer opportunities for an infinite variety of strokes. In this medieval arena of hazards and chases the tactical skill and applied psychology of an agile mind count for as much as physical fitness. The experience of age can challenge the stamina of youth on level terms. Tennis may become a life-long addiction. Developed and refined down the centuries, the complexities and subtleties of the game are inexhaustible in a single lifetime. Today there are said to be thirty different methods of serving. As one professional remarked on his eightieth birthday: 'I have been playing tennis for more than sixty years now, and I reckon I know about half of it.'[2]

An assessment of the game's physical and mental challenge

made by the Secretary of the leading London club in the early nineteenth century runs as follows:

> In the enumeration of the qualities required to place a man among the first rank of Players, should be included, strength combined with activity, great flexibility of body, force and pliancy of wrist, quickness of eye, self-possession, perseverance, temper, and judgment; and to these should be added a mind full of resources, quick to discover the weakest part of his adversary's game and to apply his own peculiar powers to the best advantage: for the body and mind, at Tennis, are equally upon the stretch, and as the hurry of the action is unfavorable to the reflective part of the game, it is the last and most difficult acquirement,to recollect, in the vehemence of execution, what it may be most judicious to endeavour to execute.[3]

It is small wonder that a game making such demands should receive a ready and enduring welcome in university towns like Oxford and Cambridge, where prowess at sport has always been prized. An activity in which body and mind are 'equally upon the stretch' was seen to offer an engaging and healthy form of relaxation from sterner studies; so that over a period of more than five hundred years successive generations of dons and undergraduates have found themselves unable to resist the invitation: 'Come, let's clear up our brows: shall we to tennis?'[4]

Appreciation has not been confined to players. Scholars have also been drawn to tennis as spectators, and the game has attracted the attention of poets from Gower and Shakespeare onwards. In Cambridge the game has been celebrated in ecstatic doggerel, beginning and ending:

*To see Good Tennis! What diviner joy
Can fill our leisure, or our minds employ?*

*Let other people play at other things;
The King of Games is still the Game of Kings.*[5]

Another attraction has been the esoteric nature of a recreation traditionally available only to the privileged few. Tennis was once indeed 'the Game of Kings'. From the fourteenth to the mid-sixteenth centuries repressive statutes, frequently repeated, prohibited the playing of ball games by common people. The motivation behind this legislation was partly sumptuary and partly the defence of the realm. The lower orders in society were not to be permitted to ape their betters; and they were to take their exercise in the practice of archery, which would benefit their country in time of war.

In 1365 Edward III made playing games an offence punishable by imprisonment. An Act of Richard II ordained that 'Servants shall use only Bows and Arrows, and leave idle Games'.[6] Under Henry IV all labourers and servants were enjoined to 'utterly leave playing at the Balls, as well Hand Ball as Foot Ball'.[7] A re-enactment under Edward IV went so far as to blame tennis and other games for causing impoverishment and leading to 'many Murders, Robberies and other heinous Felonies'.[8] These alarming allegations were repeated early in Henry VIII's reign, and an even more serious charge added: the safety of the realm was held to be imperilled by the decay of skill in archery, largely owing to the 'custumable usaige of Tenys Play, Bowls, Classhe [skittles] and other unlawful games'; whereby 'grete impoverisshement hath ensued'.[9]

The use of such strong language and the evident need for constant re-enactment of this legislation are evidence both of the popularity of the outlawed games and of a general flouting of the law.

This was certainly the case in Oxford, where there was perhaps more excuse than elsewhere. The example set by those who made the laws was scarcely conducive to obedience by others, particularly those studying at the universities, who may have believed themselves entitled to exemption as a privileged class. Henry VII and Henry VIII – and doubtless the athletic young Edward IV – were themselves keen players.

Abroad – in Scotland, in Spain and above all in France – a similar situation prevailed. In 1369 Charles V of France, himself well-known to be an ardent tennis-player, issued an edict banning games of every kind throughout his dominions. Such was the addiction of one of his successors, Francis I, that he built four courts at various of his palaces and another on a battleship. Thus on both sides of the Channel, for more than two centuries, kings with their courtiers and nobility – and not excluding clergy – practised the game enthusiastically while threatening dire penalties on commoners who might succumb to temptation and presume to disport themselves in like manner.

In England no heinous felonies attributable to tennis are known, but a murder on court was reported from Dublin, and in Rome the famously irascible painter Caravaggio settled an argument by killing his opponent. In England the most serious recorded act of tennis violence occurred at Hampton Court, when a dispute over a point led to the heir to the throne (Henry, Prince of Wales) receiving a sharp blow on the head from the racket of his opponent, the young Earl of Essex (subsequently Parliament's commander-in-chief in the Civil Wars).

At Oxford no instance of poor sportsmanship carried to criminal lengths remains on the record. Nor was tennis blamed for any of the sporadic outbursts of civil commotion in medieval times, although played by both town and gown in defiance of the law. In

1595 it was a Shrovetide match, not at tennis but at football, which resulted in a memorable brawl in High Street.

The accusation of 'grete impoverisshement' may have more force. It arose from another lure associated with the game: gambling. Among players and spectators alike, tennis established itself from early days as a vehicle for betting; much as dicing was and horse-racing was to become. Bets were placed not only on games, sets and matches but on individual points, and this is believed to account for the peculiar method of scoring adopted and still in use.

At a time when sixty rather than a hundred was widely taken to represent a whole (as in sixty minutes to the hour) the coinage in France was sexagesimal. There were sixty sous to the *double d'or*, and the *quinzaine* was a fifteen-sou piece. This was a small coin which could readily be wagered on each point, so that fifteen sous were won or lost on the first, thirty on the second, forty-five on the third (abbreviated to forty in later scoring), and a whole *double d'or* on the game at sixty. As well as four points to a game, there were originally four games to a set.

Prodigious sums were sometimes won or lost in tennis courts. Even with his own marker, Henry VIII was a heavy loser, as the chronicler Edward Hall and the royal household accounts testify. During the reign of Elizabeth I it was reported that Henry Wriothesley, third Earl of Southampton, 'hath lately lost 18,000 crowns at tennis in Paris'.[10] An extreme case in the next century was that of Baptist Noel, third Viscount Campden, who, on the occasion of his marriage in 1632, received a wedding present of £3000 for his bride from Charles I and lost £2500 of it at tennis in a single day.

This was an aspect of the game understandably frowned upon by university authorities. Standing *in loco parentis*, they acknowledged a duty to ensure that their young charges did not fall into debt. Gambling, moreover, usually involved mixing in dubious company; it attracted non-playing undesirables to the courts. In 1688 one college tutor felt obliged to issue a severe warning against student participation in tennis on this as well as other grounds. He advised that an undergraduate should refrain from frequenting public places such as bowling greens, racket courts, etc., 'for beside the danger of firing his blood by a fever, heightening passion into cursing and swearing, he must unavoidably grow acquainted with promiscuous company.'[11]

Tennis Play (c. 1700)

Among the promiscuous company, moreover, were no doubt some who did not scruple to take unfair advantage of undergraduate innocence. Nationally, cheating had become so widespread that it demanded the attention of the law. In 1664 it was enacted that persons winning money by deceit at games and sports, such as cards, dice, horse-racing and tennis, should forfeit three times the amount so won.[12]

An Intellectual and Unlawful Pastime

The encouragement of idleness was another charge laid at tennis's door. In *Abuses stript and whipt* (1622) the poet George Wither confessed to a period of indolence as a freshman at Magdalen and described how he only got down to work after

> *Having this experience, and withall*
> *Achieved some cunning with the Tennis-ball.*

A few years later, in describing 'a meere young Gentleman of the Universitie' (who had come up only for fencing and dancing, taverns and tennis), John Earle, a Fellow of Merton, identified the two marks of his seniority as 'the bare Velvet of his gowne, and his proficiencie at Tennis, where when hee can once play a Set, he is a Fresh-man no more'.[13]

What then were the origins of this distraction from learning which fired the blood and stretched the mind; and when did the townsmen and students of Oxford first taste the forbidden pleasures of the Game of Kings?

CHAPTER 2
Origins and Growth

FRANCE was the country of origin. This is evident from the terminology, for much of which there is no English equivalent: *dedans, tambour, grille, bandeau, deuce (à deux)* and *bisque*, for example. Otherwise tennis's infant years are buried in obscurity. Ball games of various kinds are known to have been played in ancient Egypt, Greece and Rome and, later, in pagan Europe and Central America, but what can be identified with certainty as tennis first emerged in France in the early part of the twelfth century as *le jeu de paume* (the game of the palm of the hand), the name by which it is still known in France today.

In the beginning this term is likely to have covered a number of different forms of hand-ball played out of doors: some in open fields (*longue paume*), others in enclosed areas such as town streets, monastery cloisters and castle courtyards (*courte paume*). Which of the versions and venues came first – and whether cloister tennis was usually played in the garth or under the arcades (or in either according to the season) – are questions as yet unresolved. There is evidence of ball play in medieval streets, but some of the earliest references are ecclesiastical and associated with religious ceremonies at Easter. A case has been also made for the game's development from an event between two teams in medieval tournaments, known as the Passage of Arms, but this has been dismissed as too late in date. In the configuration of modern courts the penthouses may represent the sloping roofs of either cloisters or houses; the dedans and side galleries are most strongly reminiscent of cloisters; yet the grille appears to represent a serving hatch and the tambour an intruding buttress, both more suggestive of a secular courtyard.

The origin of the name 'tennis' has been much debated. Although never used in France itself, it is first found in connection with the introduction of the game to Florence by a party of French knights in 1325. It was then reported that a Florentine played *palla* with them, and that this was the first occasion when *tenes* was played in those parts.[1] The now generally accepted explanation of the name is the presumed use of the word *'Tenez!'* ('Play!') called by the server to alert the receiver that play was about to commence. This has survived in the records only in its Latin forms: *'Accipe!'* and *'Excipe!'*.

From France the game spread to all parts of Europe, most notably to Italy as *giuoco della palla* (where the rules provided for contingencies such as the ball being carried away on a passing cart); to Spain (where black balls were used against white walls); and to Germany (where by the sixteenth century at least forty-six towns boasted at least one *Ballhaus*). In Scotland the game was introduced from Flanders during the thirteenth century as *caitche* or *caitchspeel* (the game of the chase), and it is likely to have crossed the Channel from France to England at about the same time. The thirteenth-century chronicler William Fitzstephen refers to London schoolboys playing *lusum pilae celebrem* in the fields annually on Shrove Tuesday;[2] which the Elizabethan antiquary Stow interpreted as tennis, but other evidence demonstrates that it would have been football.

During this period the game was flourishing in the cloisters of French seminaries and monastic schools, and not only among students. The canons who taught them played, and even *les docteurs régents*. Bishops and archbishops too were not above joining in a game during Christmas and Easter festivities.[3]

The unity of the Church in medieval Europe suggests the likelihood that clerics who had enjoyed this form of exercise in France were among the first to bring tennis to England. The game's ecclesiastical and academic provenance thus raises the possibility of play at Oxford during the university's beginnings, at a time when there were strong links with Paris and much intercourse between English and continental scholars travelling between the various centres of learning in Christendom. There is, however, no supporting evidence for this supposition.

That cloisters were used for tennis in England in the mid-fifteenth century, and not only by clerics, is known from the following indignant declaration by the bishop and dean and chapter at Exeter: 'Atte which tymes and in especiall in tyme of dyvyne service, ungoodly ruled peple most custumabely yong peple of the saide Comminalte within the saide cloistre have exercised unlawfull games as the toppe, queke [chess or draughts], penny prykke and most atte tenys, by the which the walles of the saide Cloistre have be defowled and the glas wyndowes all to brost, as it openly sheweth. . .'.[4]

Games of tennis in monasteries such as Oseney and Rewley abbeys in Oxford may not have been uncommon. At Humberstone Abbey in Lincolnshire, for example, an episcopal visitation shortly before its dissolution formally reprimanded the monks themselves for neglecting their duties in favour of tennis.

The first literary references in English, providing evidence of a wide acquaintance with the game, date from the end of the fourteenth century. In Chaucer's *Troilus and Criseyde* (c. 1385), when Troilus is advised by Pandarus to love another and let Criseyde go, tennis appears to be used as a metaphor in the line: 'But kanstow pleyen raket to and fro'; but this reference may rather be to a game by that name played with dice.[5] The name of the game itself – and in a form very close to *tenez* – makes its earliest surviving appearance a few years later in John Gower's *In Praise of Peace* (c. 1400):

> *Of the Tenetz to winne or lese a chace*
> *Mai no lif wite er that the bal be ronne;*
> *Al stant in god, what thing men schal pourchace,*
> *Thende is in him er that it be begonne.*[6]

Other early (fifteenth-century) forms of what was to become standardised as 'tennis' were 'teneys', 'tenyse', 'tenys', 'tennys' and 'tenyce', but the Latin version in general use by scholars at that time was a translation of the French *le jeu de paume*: *ludus pilae palmariae*. Later the Greek-derived 'sphaeromachy' or 'sphaeromachia' (ball contest) came into occasional use, but 'tennis' continued to be the name commonly applied in English-speaking countries until the twentieth century. Then the word progressively came to be appropriated as the abbreviated name of the modern and better known game of lawn tennis.

An English invention dating from the 1860s and first named Sphairistike, lawn tennis was devised as a simplified, out-of-door version of *courte paume*. Lost in its transfer to Victorian lawns was the intellectual challenge provided by the two salient features and crowning glories of the parent game: the hazards and the chases.

Today these terms are understood by few, but Gower's reference to the chase as a point held in abeyance, the outcome being known only to God until the play-off, suggests that this unique characteristic of the game was familiar to many among the literate in England six hundred years ago. By Elizabethan times both 'hazard' and 'chase' appear to have established themselves in common parlance in the specialised sense applied to them in tennis. There are six references to the game in Shakespeare's plays, implying not only that Shakespeare himself was knowledgeable about its finer points, but also that references to its technical terms were likely to be understood by his audiences: groundlings and all.

The most famous of these passages records Henry V's ungracious acknowledgment of a handsome, but insulting, gift of tennis balls from the Dauphin of France (where the best balls were made). This story may not be wholly fanciful because it was lifted from the works of Thomas Otterbourne, who lived and wrote during Henry V's reign.

> We are glad the Dauphin is so pleasant with us;
> His present and your pains we thank you for:
> When we have match't our rackets to these balls,
> We will, in France, by God's grace, play a set
> Shall strike his father's crown into the hazard.
> Tell him he hath made a match with such a wrangler
> That all the courts of France will be disturb'd
> With chases.[7]

The threat in this riposte may have been made good in battle at Agincourt, but when Henry's crown passed to his unwarlike son it was the French who played a real set in England. In August 1457, after landing at Sandwich and sacking the town, they treated themselves to a game of tennis (*ad tenesiam luserunt*) before re-embarking.[8]

Charles d'Orléans, while a prisoner of war in England after his capture at Agincourt, composed the first known poem devoted to the game. In it the duke, who spent more than twenty-five years in captivity while two courts at the château at Blois awaited him at home, wistfully compared life to a game of tennis:

> *J'ay tant joué avecques Aage*
> *A la paulme, que maintenant*
> *J'ay quarante-cinq sur bon gage...*[9]

The idea of the world as a tennis court and human beings as tennis balls buffeted to and fro by the rackets of fate became a much favoured literary and moralising conceit. In Webster's *Duchess of Malfi* (1612), for example: 'We are merely the stars' tennis-balls, struck and bandied Which way please them.'[10] In Sir Philip Sidney's *Arcadia* (c. 1579) mankind 'are but like tenisbals, tossed by the racket of the higher powers'.[11] And in a sermon published in 1658: 'Thus like a tennis-ball is poor man racketed from one temptation to another, till at last he hazard eternal ruine.'[12]

While knowledge of the mysteries of tennis and its special features was becoming more and more widespread, the game itself was being transformed by the evolution of the racket – by far the most important development in its long history. The art, the skill, the excitement of tennis was, by degrees, vastly enhanced through the adoption of more and more powerful means of propulsion, each stage resulting in an ever greater increase in ball control and the pace of the game.

In the beginning the ball was struck with the bare hand. A glove was then introduced for protection, as in modern fives. This became a double glove, on which cords or tendons came to be stretched across the palm like the strings of a violin bow. Next a short handle was added, and this led in turn to the invention of the *battoir*, made of wood, somewhat akin to a modern table-tennis bat. The handle was then lengthened, until the forerunner of the weapons used in all modern racket-and-ball games – a long-handled racket (or racquet) strung with sheep's gut – came into use before the close of the fifteenth century.

This heralded a long period of transition. Many players were unable to afford the luxury of a racket, and some who could preferred to stick to the customary hand or *battoir*. Towards the end of the sixteenth century old men were bemoaning, as always, how the game had changed during their lifetime.

Chapter 2

The Moat Court at Windsor Castle (c. 1500)

England, as so often, seems to have been slow to join the rest of Europe and adapt to an advance in technology. Even high-born players disdained to equip themselves with rackets like their continental counterparts. During his stay at Windsor in 1506 the King of Castile is recorded as playing a game against the Marquis of

Dorset in 'the Tennys playe' in the castle's dry moat. The king was equipped with a racket, while the marquis used his hands and received a handicap of fifteen – the inadequacy of which must have ensured victory for the distinguished guest, as diplomacy and politeness required.

The rival merits of hand and racket became a subject of scholarly discourse. In Erasmus's Colloquy on tennis, written for his students in Paris in 1522, the following exchange occurs:

NICOLAUS: Minus sudabitur, si ludamus reticulo.
HYERONIMUS: Imo reticulum piscatoribus relinquamus; elegantius est palma uti.[13]

('We shall sweat less if we play with a net [racket]'. 'Let us leave the net to fishermen. Using the hand is more seemly.')

According to Erasmus's contemporary, the Spanish humanist Juan Luis Vives, the hand was still in use by the King of Castile's subjects thirty years after the king himself had flaunted his racket among the hand-ball players at Windsor. Whether this was for reasons of poverty, class distinction or stubborn adherence to tradition is not stated. Also revealed incidently by Vives is the fact that in Paris the adoption of the racket, 'woven with strings such as are found on a six-stringed lyre', was accompanied by the introduction of smaller and harder balls. These were stuffed with dog's hair, not (as in Vives's home town of Valencia) with woollen rags.[14]

Balls were traditionally made of sheepskin stuffed with such woollen trimmings, but when wool became too expensive it was replaced in England by human hair in a leather covering. Thus Claudio in *Much Ado About Nothing*: 'the barber's man hath been seen with him; and the old ornament of his cheek hath already stuffed tennis balls.'[15] Subsequently, as rackets grew sturdier, balls were made larger, not smaller.

In England the racket slowly ousted the use of the hand in the course of the sixteenth century. There is a reference to 'the rakketters in tennyse play' dated 1581,[16] and in the following century tennis courts began to be described alternatively as racket courts (not to be confused with rackets courts, a later and different kind of building). Yet old practices persisted, at least among the young, as revealed in verses on the tennis ball published in 1612:

> *The Tennis-ball, when strucken to the ground,*
> *With Racket, or the gentle School-boies hand,*
> *With greater force, doth back againe rebound* . . .[17]

When the racket finally won acceptance as the sole weapon to be employed in orthodox tennis, hand-ball found itself a new name, 'fives', the earliest use of which can be traced to 1636.[18] Fives and hand-ball then became synonymous, and there can be little doubt that some of the earlier and cruder forms of tennis played with the hand more closely resembled what would nowadays be described as fives than tennis as it is played today. This is a point of some relevance in identifying the nature of college ball games played in Oxford in the sixteenth and seventeenth centuries.

Erasmus's use of the Latin word *reticulum* for 'racket' suggests loose stringing. Later, in France in the eighteenth century, the making and stringing of rackets became recognised as an art,[19] but it was not until the middle of the nineteenth that a modern standard of tautness was achieved by threading the horizontal strings through the vertical instead of winding them round. Meanwhile the handle had gradually reached its modern length and the gut become thicker and tougher.

The laws of tennis in modern times place no restriction on the size or shape of rackets. Normally they weigh between thirteen and eighteen ounces and are a little over two feet in length with an asymmetrical, pear-shaped head. The frame is made of ash with a splice, or middlepiece, of willow, lime or beech. Wielded by a strong player when a force is required, they can propel a ball at well over 100 miles per hour – a speed inconceivable to players of the game in past centuries.

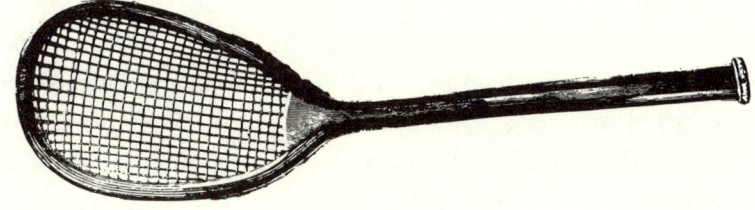

A 19th-Century Racket

When lawn tennis's much wider popularity led to the general use of 'tennis' as an abbreviation for that version of the game, the relatively little-known historic game was forced into a gradual surrender of its name to avoid confusion. In Britain it came to be known as real tennis (real in the ambiguous sense of either 'real' or 'royal'); in Australia as royal tennis; and in the USA as court tennis. Those addicted to old-fashioned Oxford slang have been known to distinguish the two more simply as 'lawners' and 'realers'.

Officials, purists and older players, however, prefer to retain traditional nomenclature. The governing body in Britain is still The Tennis and Rackets Association, and the university club at Oxford remains the Oxford University Tennis Club.

CHAPTER 3

The Golden Age

TENNIS'S golden age dawned in the sixteenth century and drew to a close at the end of the seventeenth. During that period the popularity of the game was everywhere at its peak. In the enlightenment of the Renaissance a sport which had been reserved by law for the privileged classes of nobility and clergy established itself throughout western Europe as a desirable ingredient in every young gentleman's upbringing and in every male citizen's choice of recreation.

In England the royal will faltered towards the end of Henry VIII's reign, when yet another re-enactment of the widely ignored statutes outlawing tennis and other games exempted owners of land worth £100 a year and permitted licenced courts.[1] But repression was again the order of the day under Mary Tudor: in 1555 an Act was passed 'to make voyde dyvers lycences of Houses wherein unlawfull Games be used'.[2]

This was officialdom's last fling, for public demand had already burst through the barrier of legal restraints. Tennis owed its freedom to its universal appeal. The popularity of the game had in the end proved irresistible; in the new age of the Renaissance it could be suppressed no longer. Over a period of two centuries its triumph was celebrated by all classes on both sides of the Channel. What had been a minority sport, and was to become so again, was then enjoyed by all.

In 1558, for example, a French traveller in England reported: 'Here you may commonly see artisans, such as hatters and joiners, playing at tennis for a crown, which is not to be seen elsewhere, particularly on a working day.'[3] In France the game even breached class barriers: 'the sweating together' of noblemen and peasants there was noted by Thomas Dekker. [4]

The French crown's little-heeded edicts banning all games had been similarly swept aside in a nationwide mania for tennis. Sir Robert Dallington, a secretary at the English embassy in Paris who travelled through France in about 1590, estimated that in that country there were twice as many tennis courts as churches and as many tennis-players among the poor as ale-drinkers in England.

He observed an 'infinite number of Tennis Courts throughout the land', where sets were played 'in the heat of Summer and height of the day, when others were scarce able to stirre out of dores'. More tennis was played in France than 'in all Christendome besides'. 'Me thinks it is also strange,' he went on, 'how apt they be here to play well, that ye would think they were born with Rackets in their hands, even the children themselves manage them so well, and some of the women also.' Sir Robert observed, too, that the balls in France then were covered in cloth, 'which fashion they have held this seven yeres; before which time they were of lether, like ours'. [5]

The Venetian ambassador at the French court during the same period calculated the number of courts in Paris alone as 1800. Allowance should perhaps be made for Venetian hyperbole, but other estimates ranged from as high as 1100 to no lower than 250. Even if these included playing fields for *longue paume* and unroofed buildings with plain walls, the total is still extraordinary. Dallington did not even attempt an estimate: 'I know not how many hundred there be in Paris.'

The general enthusiasm for tennis in France had extended naturally to the universities, as graphically recorded by Rabelais in his fictional account of the rage for the 'bel exercise de la paulme'

Chapter 3

A 17th-Century Paris Court

among law students at Orléans, where sixty courts were available to them. In *Pantagruel* (1532) his hero's university career was more notable for acclaim as a tennis champion than for attendance at classes in the law school. If Rabelais is to be believed, every student at Orléans was equipped with a racket and expected to graduate as a good tennis-player and an accomplished dancer, some slight acquaintance with the law being regarded as a bonus:

> *In his hand is always a racket,*
> *Or his tennis-ball in his placket:*
> *In dance he neatly can trip it;*
> *And for law, it is all in his tippet.*[6]

The high regard in which the game was held among intellectuals is abundantly documented. In later years Rousseau and Goethe praised it, and it features both in More's *Utopia* and Swedenborg's vision of Heaven. Among seventeenth-century Oxford philosophers Thomas Hobbes, a graduate of Magdalen Hall, played tennis to keep fit in old age (playing at the age of 75, according to Aubrey); and John Locke, a Christ Church man, demonstrated at least his familiarity with the game by using the ball to illustrate a point in metaphysics:

> A Tennis-ball, whether in Motion by the stroke of a Racket, or lying at rest, is not by any one taken to be a *free Agent*. If we enquire into the reason, we shall find it is because we conceive not a Tennis-ball to think, and consequently not to have any Volition, or preference of Motion to rest, or *vice versa.* [7]

The gambling associated with tennis caused it to be frowned upon by some moralists, but the game was defended even on that count by the Spaniard Vives, who lectured at Oxford as a Reader in Humanity and, when not (as frequently) *in absentia*, had rooms at Corpus. The purpose behind his dialogue published in *Leges Ludi* (1539) was to deter a younger generation from warlike activities like archery and attract them towards peaceful sport. His advice to students was that any game was zestless without a stake, but that no stake should be a big one lest it disturb the mind while playing and vex and torture it: 'That is not a game,' he wrote; 'it is rather the rack.' [8]

A different view was taken by Laurence Humfrey DD, a notably pious President of Magdalen; but even he refrained from condemning tennis 'if honest pleasure, not filthy gayne be sought' (and oaths not uttered). [9]

Thus throughout the sixteenth century this recently unlawful activity won the general approval of the great and the good. Most pertinently for Oxford, it was awarded high marks by those who taught in universities and highly commended by those who advised and pontificated on the welfare of students and the correct methods of raising the sons of the nobility and gentry.

Erasmus in his Colloquy declared nothing to be better than tennis for exercising every part of the body, and this view was fully endorsed by Thomas Coghan of Oriel, 'Master of Artes and Bacheler of Physicke', who went so far as to claim the support of Galen, the father of medical science (*c*. AD 130–201). The subject of Coghan's *The Haven of Health*, published in 1584, was avoidance of the plague in Oxford. Apart from fleeing the city ('with speed to goe farre off from the place infected'), the best remedy he could prescribe for Oxford's endangered scholars was a regular regimen of frequent exercise,[10] and:

> ... above all other kindes of exercises, Galen most commendeth the play with the little ball, which we call Tenise

... chiefly for that it doth exercise all parts of the body alike, as the legges, armes, necke, head, eies, back and loynes, and delighteth greatly the minde, making it lusty and cheereful. All which commodities may be found in no other kind of exercise ... wherefore those founders of Colleges are highly to be praysed, that have erected Tenyse courtes for the exercise of their Scholers: and I counsaile all students as much as they may to use that pastime.[11]

In his *Boke Named the Governour* (1531) Sir Thomas Elyot also applauded tennis as admirable exercise for young men, but warned that it was more strenuous than archery, not being an individual sport at which a man could stop if he became overtired: 'Two men play ... Wherefore neither of them is at liberty to measure the exercise.'[12]

English humanists of this period were wont to take their lead from Italy, and an English translation of Castiglione's influential manual, *Il Cortegiane*, was published in 1561. This conveyed to the Elizabethan upper class the Italian cachet of approval of tennis as exercise befitting a courtier. It was followed by the publication of similarly influential works by two leading English educationists. In *The Scholemaster* (1570) Roger Ascham encouraged his pupils to 'use and delight in all courtly exercises, and gentlemanly pastimes' such as tennis.[13] In *Positions* (1581) Richard Mulcaster, while also recommending tennis for exercise ('this playing abateth grossenes and corpulence'), makes an interesting distinction between play facing an opponent and play 'against a wall alone to exercise the body with both the hands in every kind of motion'.[14]

Evidence that aptitude at tennis was considered an appropriate accomplishment for aspiring young gentlemen in Oxford as early as the beginning of the sixteenth century (when play was still forbidden to the lower orders) comes from some exercises set at that time by the Master of Magdalen College School. Pupils included choristers and other junior members of the college, sons of Oxford citizens and boarders from elsewhere, all aged between ten and eighteen. One of the sentences which the curriculum required them to translate into Latin was: 'Me semeth thu shotes well, thu rides well, thu pleis at tenesse well.'[15]

Even more extravagant claims were made for the game than the pleasure it gave and the medical benefits and social advantages it was deemed to bestow. The notion that tennis qualified as an activity superior to a mere game was advanced by Antonio Scaino, an Italian monk who sought to elevate it to the status of both a science and an art. In his treatise on the subject, written in 1555 at the command of the Duke of Ferrara (a keen player), he argued on behalf of this 'very noble and rare exercise so beneficial for body and mind and especially of benefit in the purification of the spirits through which the soul performs all its functions, even that of understanding' an equality with medicine, music and mathematics on the one hand and rhetoric, poetry, grammar and dialectics on the other.[16]

Two hundred years later this high praise received some measure of support from the Royal Academy of Sciences in France when it recognised tennis as the only game fit to be described as an art.[17]

Popularisation did not supersede royal patronage. The two went hand in hand, enthusiastic play by Bourbon and Stuart monarchs continuing unabated. Among the French kings who were known devotees, Henry II was reputed to be of championship class; Charles IX, pictured racket in hand at the age of two, is said to have played for six hours a day; and Henry IV (of Navarre) is likely to have been a characteristically formidable performer on court.

In England Elizabeth I was an interested spectator. Early Stuart kings had played the game in Scotland, and James VI and I, although no games-player himself, recommended them, including 'playing at the caitch or tennise', to his heir – not only for the sake of fitness, but also for 'the banishing of idleness, the mother of all vice'.[18] Prince Henry followed this advice so ardently that strait-laced courtiers were shocked to behold the heir to two thrones 'sweating like an artisan'.

His brother, Charles I, played the game in Whitehall until the outbreak of civil war forced him to move to Oxford. At this a London pamphleteer breathed a Deep Sigh that among the 'Miseries of the Pallace' there was now 'no racket nor balling in the Tenis court': Whitehall had not only 'A Pallace without a Presence!' but also 'A Court without a Court!'[19]

Fortunately, the court was not without a court in its new capital. On the afternoon of 27 December 1642, as the local historian, antiquary and gossip, Anthony Wood, succinctly noted: 'Rupert at Mr Edwards his tennis court, and so was the king.' Uncle and nephew were again playing in this court (in Oriel Street) the following morning when a messenger from Parliament arrived with proposals for articles of accommodation: 'A trumpeter came into Oxford from my lord of Essex, about some new tidings, and the lordes repayred to his majestie to the tennice court, where the business was imparted to him.'[20]

So important was tennis to King Charles that in November of the following year his Master of the Robes was instructed to obtain a new tennis suit for him from enemy-occupied London. Application was accordingly made to Parliament for a pass to permit a groom and his servant to travel from London to Oxford 'with 4 dozen of gloves, which are much wanted by His Majesty,

The Future King James II on Court

and 4 yards of taby [silk taffeta] to be a tennis-suit, and 2 pairs of garters and roses with silk buttons and other necessaries for making up of the said suit.'[21]

In those times armed hostilities were evidently thought no good reason for rejecting a reasonable request. After due consideration Parliament sportingly obliged with the required permission so that His Majesty might not suffer the indignity of being seen improperly dressed on an Oxford court. Indeed it may be confidently asserted that no tennis-player in Oxford has ever been more handsomely attired.

The later Stuarts too were addicted to the game. Charles II played regularly at six o'clock in the morning in Whitehall, where 'to see how the King's play was extolled, without any cause at all, was a loathsome sight'. This forthright observation was made by Samuel Pepys, who added, however: 'though sometimes indeed he did play very well and deserved to be commended'.[22] According to the diarist, it was the king's custom to weigh himself before and after playing and to judge whether or not his game had been a good one by the amount of weight lost.[23]

James II, the last of the Stuart kings to rule, was playing tennis by the age of eight. When he lost his crown, Louis XIV considerately allowed him to take up residence at the palace of St Germain-en-Laye, where the consolation of two tennis courts was available to fill the empty days of exile.

CHAPTER 4

Early Days in Oxford

TENNIS made its first recorded appearance in Oxford during the dark ages when games-playing was still a criminal offence. In 1450 Thomas Blake, a skinner, William Whyte, a barber, and John Waryn, a glover, were summoned before Master Gilbert Kymer (Chancellor of the university and Commissary General of the Bishop of Lincoln) and Professor J. Beek on a charge of illicit play. With their hands on the Holy Gospels, the accused were forced to abjure the game of tennis (*ludum tenesiarum*) within the city of Oxford and its precincts.[1]

The record of this prosecution is in Latin with the exception of the single word, 'husbundemen', used to describe all three tradesmen. The meaning of husbandmen in this context is 'householders', and its significance here may relate to one of the provisions of the statutes prohibiting games. This imposed harsher penalties on those who, whether or not themselves players, allowed their premises to be used for this nefarious purpose. In the eyes of the law, keeping a tennis court was more reprehensible than keeping a brothel.

The Act of Richard II against 'idle Games', as confirmed by re-enactment under Henry IV in 1410, made offenders liable to six days in prison and penalised mayors, sheriffs and constables who defaulted in the exercise of their powers of enforcement. The absence in this case of any mention of a fine, let alone imprisonment as provided for by the law, suggests a reluctance to prosecute, or at any rate a policy of leniency, on the part of the university authorities who ruled the town.

Later evidence indicates that an official turning of blind eyes to evasions of this law was widespread. It seems that in the fifteenth and early sixteenth centuries local authorities chose to treat the playing of tennis in much the same way as those in the early 1990s treated Sunday trading: it was too popular and harmless for the law to be enforced with any vigour. Central government was relatively powerless and out of step with local sentiment.

Thus in Oxford the practice of keeping courts in defiance of the law continued. In 1497 John Warleman, a parishioner of St Mary Magdalen, was 'presented' (prosecuted) for using his premises for tennis and other unlawful games – *le Tenyse & alia joca illicita. Diversos homines ludentes ad pilam vocat.* His punishment is not on the record. [2]

Again, in 1508, Michael Clowe, William Philips, Richard Andrewes and Henry Bushy 'that kept tenys playes and bowlinge allies' were fined sixpence each: a token sum for an offence for which the full legal penalty was by then £20 and a day in the stocks. It comes as no great surprise, therefore, to find that two of the same offenders, Clowe and Andrewes, were convicted of the very same offence seven years later, when the fine was again no more than sixpence. [3]

The courts kept by these men, and doubtless by others, catered to townsmen and members of the university alike, but a disapproving entry in Merton College's record book for April 1492 makes it plain that they were not considered suitable venues for the latter. This entry immortalises Richard Holt, a Fellow of the college, as the earliest named university tennis-player; but his rakish career serves only to illustrate the then lowly status of this forbidden pastime, frowned upon in academic circles at that time as a time-wasting diversion which attracted none but the idle and dissolute.

Holt was a young Fellow who, most unusually for that period, never took holy orders. 'Grave complaints' were made against him. He was over-familiar with his seniors and often absent from, or late for, chapel. Instead of staying in college and studying, he wandered about the town and 'frequented suspect places'. He gambled at dice. He played at tennis – and in public: *scilicet de crebro lusu ad tenesiam & hoc in locis pupplicis*. *Crebro* implies some measure of addiction. Holt, alas, was soon parted from his Fellowship and from Oxford. [4]

In 1530 the Privy Council determined that the law must be enforced and seen to be enforced in Oxford. The mayor and bailiffs were instructed to search every house in the town for unlawful games equipment and burn it publicly in the market place on a market day. A similar order was sent to the Bishop of Lincoln's Commissary (an office then held *ex officio* by the Vice-Chancellor), who was responsible for the conduct of scholars and other privileged persons.

A revealing spat between town and gown ensued. The mayor accused the Vice-Chancellor of secretly returning confiscated cards, dice, bowls, etc., to the students. In denying the charge, the Vice-Chancellor's representative retorted that 'the Mayor, Bailiffs & Chamberlains ... always do maintain openly unlawful games of tenys, as in two houses of the rent lying next to Smith Gate, one of the east side and another in the west side, taking more rent of the tenants for the maintaining of the said play yerely'. [5]

These, the earliest identifiable in Oxford, were the courts involved in the prosecutions of 1508 and 1515. The nominal sixpenny fines are therefore explained by the embarrassing fact that the town authorities who were required to enforce the law were themselves not only the landlords of the premises but even profited from their illegal use by exacting a higher rent.

Early Days in Oxford

Like Little Gate (where there was also a court), Smith Gate was one of the less important points of entry through the town walls. Located at the north end of Cat (or Catt) Street, it was a postern gate between the main entries of North Gate and East Gate. The courts were sited near the town ditch between what was pungently described as 'The Dunghill' and the octagon Lady Chapel which had been erected near the gate and survives today as Hertford College's Middle Common Room.

The east court ran north/south behind the chapel with its gateway to the chapel's north. In 1601 Henry Toldervey, who was to become mayor in 1614, was granted permission to extend the north wall by six inches and the south wall by two and a half feet into New College Lane at the cost of a payment of sixpence per annum to the city bailiffs. [6]

This court remained in use until 1690, when it was converted into two dwelling houses. The keeper in 1671 is mentioned by Anthony Wood as 'Hudson's son at the racket court neare Smith Gate'.[7] Ten years later the property was in the hands of Thomas Wood, a stonemason; for in April 1681 Richard Frogley, a carpenter, began a suit against him alleging that he had refused to pay for work done 'at a stable by the Lady's Chappell or roundhouse, and in the said Thomas Wood's rackett court'. [8] The outcome of the suit is not known, but in 1685 the City granted a new lease of the messuage and racket court to 'Thomas Woods, of the Univ. of Oxford, stone cutter'.[9] His widow Alice held it until 1694, but in the following year the messuage 'heretofore part of a Rackett Court' was leased to Henry Clements, bookseller.[10] Of the west court there is no record after 1530.[11]

A further accusation of neglect of duty in enforcing the law was levelled against the city fathers in 1575, when an appeal was made to the Privy Council by a disgruntled city bailiff who alleged that 'justices do not see that all unlawful games ... be expelled and quite put down'.[12] On that occasion, however, the complaint related specifically to dice and cards. By that date tennis had achieved respectability: courts were being licensed by the government.

On 6 March 1555 a licence was granted 'under pleasure' (that is, until revoked) 'to Henry Mylwarde of the city of Oxford to keep in his house in the said city a tennis playe for the use, recreation and occupying of all true subjects and all noblemen, gentlemen and other honest persons (vagabonds, apprentices, servants and scholars playing against their masters' wills only excepted)'.[13] This is the earliest record relating to the Oriel Street tennis court, whose walls (as rebuilt in the following century) survive to this day.

Twelve years later, on 14 April 1567, a similar licence, this time for twenty years, was granted to 'Bartholomew Lantt of Oxford, yoman'.[14] Lantt (also spelt Lant, Launt or Lante) was the leaseholder of the surviving Smith Gate court, and it is not clear whether this licence was a belated move to regularise the use of that court or whether it was his intention to built a new one, there or elsewhere. It was his son, John Lant, a Student of Christ Church, who was later to build the first court in Merton Street.

That scholars were among those specifically excluded from licensed play in the city without special permission was no doubt to keep them out of mischief, but it also reflected a change of attitude and policy on the part of the university. Since tennis was no longer condemned as an idle pursuit, but valued instead as an aid to attainment of the Juvenalian ideal of *mens sana in corpore sano*, the colleges had decided that it would be wise and proper to provide their own facilities for the exercise of ball play.

CHAPTER 5
College Ball Courts

OXFORD college statutes disallowed the playing of ball games against buildings, walls and roofs on college premises. This was a sensible precaution against noise, nuisance and broken windows, not to mention gambling, but it had the effect of driving students into the town to satisfy their appetite for exercise and recreation.

It was towards the middle of the sixteenth century, following relaxation of the anti-games laws, that the colleges came to accept the desirability of designated play areas within their own precincts. This development enabled the Laudian statutes of 1636 to confirm the century-old law excluding scholars from licensed town courts by forbidding members of the university from playing *lusus globorum* in the private yards and gardens of townsmen. Obedience to this injunction proved short-lived, however. On the passing of the Commonwealth and coming of the Restoration it was generally ignored, and from that time the need for in-college recreation dwindled as relations between gown and town grew progressively less fractious.

The delicate matter of disregarding Founders' wishes and breaching statutes was a moral problem which some colleges found harder to resolve than others. At Brasenose, whose statutes expressly forbade ball games, the Fellows wrote to the Visitor, who was Bishop of Lincoln, inquiring hopefully whether he would be agreeable to interpreting them in such a manner as to permit the erection of a tennis court (*sphaeristerion*) which they were proposing to build in College.

The bishop replied helpfully that he was 'verie inclinable' to the request, 'for though bodily exercise profitt nothing to merit in religion, yet it availeth much for health after intermission from studie ... Bowes and braynes if long and deeply bent, will quickly weaken or crack.' Yet, although so minded ('readie with favour'), His Lordship entreated the Fellows 'to stay a little while', craving time for deliberation 'and you shall know my mind with speed convenient'. [1]

This communication was written informally in English. Bishop Barlowe's formal adjudication after taking legal advice followed in Latin. In translation, it ran as follows:

> William, by Divine providence Bishop of Lincoln, lawfully appointed Visitor of Brasenose College within the beneficent University of Oxford, to one and all of Christ's faithful to whom the present letters of testimony have come, greetings in the Lord. In so far as, among the other laudable statutes, ordinances and regulations of the same College, it has been established and decreed, *that no Fellow or Scholar or Servant of the said College should play at dice, games of chance, cards or ball, nor engage in any other harmful, ignoble or unlawful game within the said College*: since supplication has been made to us through the Principal and Fellows of the same College, in what degree such a statute of the above-mentioned College in the matters referred to above can be interpreted by us by virtue of our authority in this particular, and for our permission to build a ball court [*sphaeristerio*] there, in so far as the above-mentioned statute allows, we deem fit to communicate to them thus. Having therefore consulted lawyers, we understand from them that, by the laws of governments and civil law, games of dice, chance and cards are not without offence, and these

games are designated and called harmful and unlawful, and are also absolutely forbidden to clergy by canon law; but ball play [*ludum pilae*] is harmless, lawful and permissible. And so, weighing carefully with due seriousness as much the intention of the statute-maker as the words of the statute, after mature deliberation we interpret, determine and declare that only that ball game which is played with battoir or racket [*pilamine seu reticula*] is prohibited by this statute, and is numbered among the harmful, ignoble and unlawful, which can in no way be engaged in by Scholars without offence, or at any rate a large measure of blame and certainly pecuniary expense. However, ball play with the hand [*pilae palmariae ludum*] is in no way prohibited, since it is practised only for the sake of bodily exercise and health. Provided that it is not played for money, and such moderation is applied that it does not pose a hindrance to studies, it cannot be harmful or unlawful; but we wish that limit to be retained and observed which the Principal of the said College, or in his absence the Vice-Principal and the two senior Fellows in residence, prescribe. And we license by the present letter the said Principal and Fellows of the above-mentioned College to build and construct, or arrange for the building of, a tennis court [*sphaeristerium*] there for the playing of hand ball [*ludo pilae palmariae*] only, and not otherwise (provided that it does not contravene the laws of the land). As evidence of this, we have authorised our episcopal seal to be placed on the present letter.

    Given at our palace at Buckden on the sixth day of April, in the year of our Lord 1609, the first year of our appointment. [2]

The terms of this ruling are of considerable interest. If the above interpretations of *pilamine* (not to be found in any dictionary) and *reticula* (literally 'netting' but used by Erasmus for racket as opposed to hand in the context of tennis) are correct, traditional tennis played with the hand was by this date considered a tame and harmless form of amusement for the young, no longer an attraction to gamblers. For serious play, and with it serious betting, the vastly superior pace and skill of the game as now played with the racket had ousted the old-fashioned use of the hand.

Owing either to reservations similar to those expressed by Brasenose's Visitor or for reasons of economy, or both, the typical Oxford college court was no more than a rudimentary version of the modern tennis court. A walled space or enclosure was located on a relatively secluded site where it would cause least disturbance to studies. Variously known in English as a ball court, tennis court or racket court and in Latin as *sphaeristerium* or *sphaeristerion* (possibly adopted from its use in Pliny the Younger's letters), it was an unroofed, paved area bounded by two, three or four walls and, like a modern school yard, available for *sphaeromachia* at any one of an assortment of games played with hand, racket or (possibly) foot. It is likely to have been intended for knocking up, practising strokes or playing simplified variations of tennis rather than the proper game in an orthodox court, the building of which would have been a substantial and expensive undertaking.

Sometimes the Latin names were even applied to open spaces without walls, as in William Williams's *Oxonia Depicta* (1733) where bowling greens at Magdalen and New College are marked with the word '*Sphaeristerion*'. Yet in university and city alike such courts and terms were customarily associated with the game of tennis. In the record of a lease in 1576, for example, a building on the east side of Vinehall Lane (now Alfred Street) is identified as 'a certain sphaeristerium called le tenys court'.[3]

Today there is a clear distinction between tennis on the one hand and games derived from it, such as fives, rackets and squash, on the other. Fives, rackets and squash courts are enclosed by plain walls and have no net. Opponents stand side by side and play the ball alternately against the front wall facing them. The scoring is sequential. In tennis, opponents face each other on either side of a net, over which (or round which) the ball must pass. The court, the chase, the method of scoring are all distinctive. In former times no such distinction was made. Fives was not differentiated from tennis until the seventeenth century; rackets is an eighteenth-century invention (originating in debtors' gaols); and squash (properly squash rackets) is a nineteenth-century soft-ball derivative of rackets. In each case the formulation of standardised rules came even later.

So in modern terminology most of the Oxford college ball courts might more appropriately be designated as fives or rackets courts. None of the few surviving illustrations of them shows a net; although the more elaborate of them are likely to have been divided, as were the college courts at Cambridge, by at least a simple, unobtrusive cord, with or without the suspended fringe which was the fashion at that time. But that these courts were called tennis courts and their intended use was for the practice of what was then known as tennis is not in doubt.

The first recorded college court in England, built for the playing of *pila palmaria*, dates from the 1470s. It was not at Oxford, but at Corpus Christi College, Cambridge, which at that date must have obtained a special licence. Subsequent improvements kept Corpus men up to date with the game. The walls were heightened around 1500; the whole court was replaced by another during the sixteenth century; and a roof to this new court was added in 1633.

College courts at Cambridge are more fully documented than

those at Oxford; and, although one would have expected the pattern at the two universities to be similar, they appear, on the available evidence, to have been constructed to higher standards and at a correspondingly higher cost. They were, in fact, more authentically tennis courts than mere ball courts. [4]

One reason behind this difference may have been the adoption by Cambridge colleges in the sixteenth century of a more determined and settled policy of providing their students with exercise and amusement in addition to food, drink and tuition. Tennis and bowls were then the approved games. Of the sixteen colleges thirteen had bowling greens and ten had tennis courts. All these courts were originally open to the sky, but, as at Corpus, some – notably those at Emmanuel, King's and Pembroke – were covered at a later date. At Oxford no college courts are known to have been roofed.

The Cambridge game was *le jeu quarré*, not *le jeu à dedans*. Courts featured *l'ais* (the grille) and *le petit trou*, but no dedans – a form which may still be seen at the Falkland Palace court in Scotland. Their dimensions usually ran to the full size (approximately ninety by thirty-six feet), the length being divided by a cord hanging from a height of five feet at the sides to two and a half in the middle (lower than today); but there was no complete uniformity. The views of the colleges by David Loggan (1690) show, for example, side penthouses and galleries at Emmanuel but none at St John's.

The Order Book of Emmanuel College contains the only surviving record of rules for the use of a college court at either university and may well have been typical of both.

> Oct.29.1651. For the better regulating of the Tenniscourt it is ordered by the Master and Fellowes *unanimi consensu*,

that the key of it shalbe in the keeping of the Deane, who is to take care that the door be kept lockt, and none suffered to play dureing the howers herafter mentioned, vizt. from one of the clock till three in the afternoone, and from eight of the clock at night till tenn the next morning; unless any of the Fellowes shall desire to play there in any of those howers, who may take any fellow commoner with them; yet soe as that they clear the court, shutt the door, and return the key to the Deane at their comeing away.[5]

At Oxford, college records contain a few references to ball courts dating from the latter half of the sixteenth century and rather more from the peak period of the seventeenth when, in the words of the Victoria County History, 'the demand among students for sport was reflected in the numerous tennis courts, bowling greens, dancing schools and cockpits built in the city during this period'.[6]

Generally, however, information is scanty and comes principally from two extraneous sources: the antiquary Anthony Wood and the topographical artist David Loggan. Loggan's *Oxonia Illustrata* was published in 1675, and the insatiably curious Wood (1632–95) was writing *Historia et Antiquitates Universitatis Oxoniensis*, *The Ancient and Present State of the City of Oxford* and the miscellanea collected in *The Life and Times of Anthony Wood* at much the same time.

Wood's interest was a personal one: his family were the proprietors of the court in Merton Street, and he was born and lived his whole life on the premises. The existence of several college courts, no record of which can be found in the colleges' own archives, are known only from a passing reference in Wood's writings.

It can thus be established that, during a period running from about 1530 to 1700, there were ball courts of some kind within the precincts of the following colleges: Balliol, Christ Church, Corpus, Exeter, Hart Hall, Jesus, Lincoln, Merton, New College, Oriel, Queen's, Pembroke, St John's and University College. The exceptions are All Souls, Brasenose, Magdalen, Trinity, Wadham and the other halls.

The three best-known Oxford courts, often referred to as the Christ Church, Merton and Oriel courts, all date from this time, but, contrary to general belief, these were never college courts. Standing on land outside the college walls, college-owned in the case of Christ Church and Merton (although not until later by Oriel), they were built, leased and operated as public courts. These three colleges all had other ball courts within their own walls for their private use.

The earliest and fullest college record comes, unexpectedly, from the account books of one of the smallest colleges, occupying a restricted site. In the words of the historian of Lincoln College:

> In the College grounds there was now a tennis court for the use of the more energetic fellows and undergraduates. Situated in the northeast corner next to Brasenose, it makes its first appearance in the accounts in 1566 when Mr. William Fairberd was paid for 'setting certain stoups on the Back-side of the colledge, with rails in the tennys-court and gardains'. We read of locks purchased for the tennis-court door in 1568, 1599 and 1618. In 1573 John Singleton hired his cart 'to carye stones into our tennys court'. Forty-four years later Edward Thornton was paid £3 6s. 8d. for repairing the tennis-court ['For 3 loades of sand for the Tennis Court, 2s. 6d.; to Thornton for Timber and Boards and his worke in the Tennis Court, £3 6s. 8d.; for 3 bushels of lime

about the Tennis Court, 2s. 0d.'] In 1660 we hear again of dirt being removed from the tennis-court.[7]

Other entries occur in 1623 ('to the carpenter and mason for the window in the tennis court, 5s. 4d.'); in 1636 ('for labourers for whelinge the dirt out of ye ball-court, 11s. 0d., to the carters for carryinge 27 loads of ye said dirt, 13s. 6d.'); and in 1648 ('for making a partition betwixt ye ball court and garden, 5s. 6d.; to ye mason for ye Ball court window, 4s. 6d.'). The amount of dirt which had to be removed from the court suggests the absence of a roof; in which case the window must have been in a wall shared with another building.

The lack of any similar record of a court within a much richer college occupying a much more spacious site is surprising. There is little likelihood that Magdalen harked back to the origins of the game and made traditional use of its cloisters. It may be that the statutes were more strictly interpreted than at Brasenose, or it may be that a college with greater space at its disposal preferred *longue paume*, thus avoiding the necessity of building walls.

It is also possible that a college with a bowling green regarded that amenity as a sufficient provision for recreation. (Magdalen's enjoyed an hour or two of fame after the fall of Oxford during the Civil Wars, when Cromwell and Fairfax celebrated with a game there. Since tennis was the Game of Kings, perhaps good republicans thought it politically correct to play a different game.)

The Magdalen accounts for 1647 record a payment *pro opere in sphaeristerio*, and those for 1678 another for *circumfodienti sphaeristerium*.[8] These payments are attributed to work undertaken in the Grove walks and meadows, not placed under the heading relating to buildings. Clearly, therefore, they refer to the college bowling green, which is marked as such by Loggan and as *sphaeristerion* in *Oxonia Depicta*.

Magdalen's statutes forbid 'flinging or shooting stones, balls, wood, earth or playing any game which would damage glass windows, walls, roofs etc.' Possibly this was interpreted as permitting bowls but not tennis – until in the late nineteenth century part of the area in front of New Buildings was laid out for lawn tennis (and, subsequently, croquet). More probably, as occurred at New College, a ball-play area was located within the grounds at a distance from the college buildings. If so, this would have been in the Grove, now the deer park, among what Agas's Plan of 1578 designates as orchards, pastures and walks. A century later Loggan shows an open walled space there, immediately to the east of the bowling green.

The discovery of tennis balls in the rafters of the halls at Wadham and Merton (now on display at the Museum of Oxford) reveals that in some colleges tennis might have been enjoyed without the benefit of a purpose-built court. These balls may be evidence of nothing more than unauthorised undergraduate high spirits, for it is hard to believe that any college would allow its hall to be cleared and windows put at risk by sanctioning its use as a ball court. On the other hand, it is possible that some form of tennis akin to badminton was occasionally permitted. At Brasenose towards the end of the nineteenth century even the college library was in regular use by the Fellows for badminton and bowls.

Of the other colleges without traceable courts, All Souls, without a body of undergraduates, is unlikely to have built one. Brasenose was not a rich college and, despite what was acknowledged as the Visitor's 'pliability with respect to the statute *de pilae ludo*',[9] the court for which the Fellows had sought permission was never built. Loggan's view of Brasenose shows a yard and wall outside the west end of the chapel, and this may have served instead as a rough-and-ready ball-play area.

Trinity, in the years after its foundation in 1555, was struggling to survive in the crumbling buildings of pre-Reformation Durham College. It may therefore, like Brasenose and Wadham (founded in 1610), not have been prepared to devote limited resources to providing its students with this facility. Moreover, in Ralph Kettell Trinity had an exceptionally austere President, and it may be that, even if affordable, no such frivolous distraction from learning as a ball court would have been countenanced during his long term of office, which stretched from 1599 to 1643.[10] But it may also be that *longue paume* was permitted in a secluded part of the college's ample grounds.

At Balliol a ball court was erected half way along the college's western perimeter wall, opposite houses on the north side of St Mary Magdalen churchyard.[11] In Loggan's view of the college it is seen as an open space with flat, bare walls; and it is also identifiable on a plan made twenty years later.[12] Only two walls are visible: a high front wall (the southern end of the college stable) and a long side wall at right angles to it, suggesting a knock-up area or a game more resembling bat-fives or pelota or jai alai than orthodox tennis. Further mentions of the court during this period appear in the college records in connection with the leasing of an adjacent tenement.[13]

An earlier and quite different kind of reference to a tennis court in Balliol's Deeds provides evidence of the opposition to sport as a potential source of noise and nuisance in or near places of learning and study. A condition of the lease of a garden owned by the college to John Hore, glover, and Agnes his wife in 1541 stipulated that they or their assigns 'shall not make nor suffre to be made any bowling alley, butts, tenes cowtre, or any other manner of pastyme shall suffre their to be used which shall or may be at any time lett, hindrance or noysome to estudients'.[14]

Chapter 5

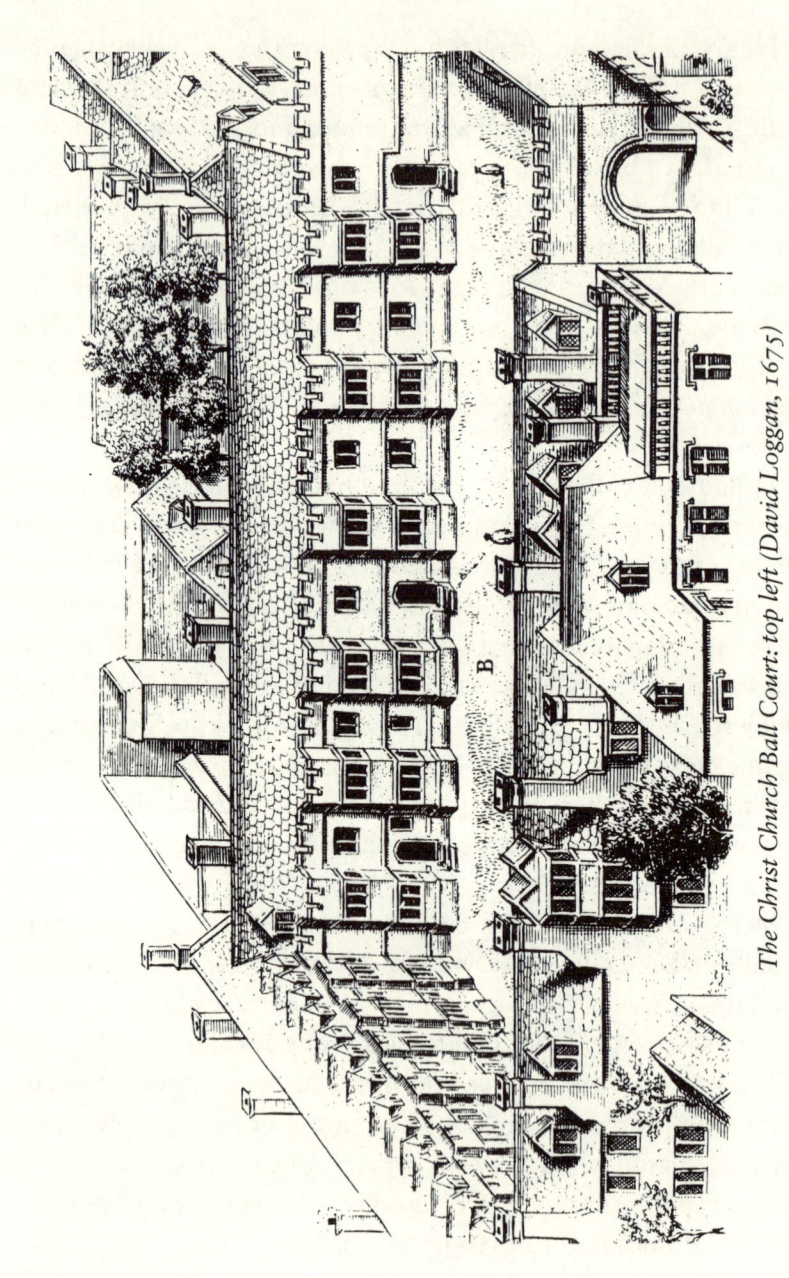

The Christ Church Ball Court: top left (David Loggan, 1675)

Since the land in question was bounded to the north by the Divinity School, this restraint is understandable; and a similar consideration may well account for the disappearance from the records of the Smith Gate west court about this date. It would have been sited inconveniently close to the north-east corner of the schools quadrangle.

The college court at Christ Church was situated to the east of the Peckwater quadrangle and north of the Canterbury quadrangle at the extreme north-east of the college boundary. Loggan's view is of a more complete and elaborate enclosure than Balliol's, with three unbroken high walls and a wide opening in the fourth.

The existence of a court at Corpus is known only from a single reference. This occurs in the college accounts for 1551/52 where the expenditure of sixpence on the making of a tennis-court door is recorded. The court is thought to have stood on the eastern side of the college on the site of the present Gentleman Commoners' buildings.

The erection of a tennis court at Exeter in September 1590 is noted in the college Register among other building work: *extructum etiam sphaeristerium*.[15] This court survived only until 1618, when Peryam's Mansions were built over its site, which was most likely located against the college's Brasenose Lane wall where the new building was later joined to the present hall. It was then referred to in the college's *Liber Implementorum* as 'a Tennys Court' – after the word 'Ball' had been deleted and 'Tennys' substituted.[16] Evidence of a replacement is to be found in the Rector's Accounts, dated 13 April 1652: 'It. to the Smyth for an hinge to the ball-court door'; but when and where this second court was built and when it was pulled down is not recorded.

At Jesus a section of the college wall abutting Ship Street was brought into play as the side wall of a ball court. Wood identifies the location of an Exeter College tenement as 'in the middle of this lane, about Jesus College ball-court'. The west wall of the Principal's garden formed the other side of the court. Both walls were 'very lofty'.[17]

Merton's perimeter walls were heightened in the north-west corner, near the west end of the chapel, and a paved floor was laid to make a court. Leather-covered balls have been found lodged in putlog holes in the chapel exterior. Loggan depicts three undergraduates playing at handball there. Their discarded caps and gowns are lying on the ground, and the game is being watched by two dons. This court is referred to by Anthony Wood when itemising the halls 'plucked downe' in the building of Corpus. Among them was 'Christopher Hall next to Merton College ball-court'.[18]

The court at New College has proved hard to discover, possibly owing to its early disappearance. Located where it might be most expected – away from the college buildings and out of sight – it occupied part of what is now the south wing of the gardens, set at right-angles to the main vista and lying between the town wall (on the east) and the graveyard of St Peter-in-the-East (on the west). In *Oxford Topography* it is stated: 'This piece of ground was once New College ball-court; in Agas it is called their orchard.'[19]

Agas's Plan of Oxford is dated 1578 – a time when fervour for tennis was at a height and more courts were beginning to be built to meet demand. A more modern replacement at a rich college like New College therefore seems likely, and Agas does indeed show a long, free-standing building with a pitched roof towards the north-west corner of the orchard. If this was not a tennis court (a well house is a possible alternative), it is possible that the governing body preferred to leave the peace of the orchard undisturbed, deciding that the proximity of the Smith Gate court at the end of New College Lane made another in college unnecessary.

Ball Play in Merton College (David Loggan, 1675)

Oriel had one of the grander courts. It was built in 1653 at a cost of £23, defrayed from an admission charge of 5s. per head imposed on commoners.[20] Its general availability to all members of the college was stressed in the Dean's Register, where it was described as *nova fabrica qua commensales et superioris et inferioris ordinis pilis lusoriis se exercerent*.[21] Like that at Christ Church, this court boasted three and a half walls, and Loggan shows a bench for spectators in the breach. It made use of the boundary wall on Grove Lane (now Magpie Lane) to the north of college's back gate and was presumably destroyed when Bishop Robinson's buildings were erected there in 1719.

Pembroke's court was similar to Merton's: two high walls at

right angles. Loggan shows these heightened walls in the southwest corner of the Master's garden. This was the central of three gardens known as the college's triple paradise. The Commoners' was to the east, and the Fellows', which included a bowling green, to the west. The dividing walls, and hence possibly the ball court, date from 1651. In 1698 leave was granted by the City for the erection of a new wall 'from the West end of the Colledge Wall to the East end of the Colledge Balcourt'.[22] A view by Michael Burghers in 1700 depicts three players watched by two dons. Since Loggan's view at least one tree had been cut down to extend the play area. In William Williams's *Oxonia Depicta* (1733) the central garden has become all sward and the ball court has disappeared.

The existence and whereabouts of the Queen's College court, otherwise unknown, is revealed incidentally by Anthony Wood when he writes of this college: 'The first habitation that the Scholars of this House had was near to the place where their Ballcourt now is, and particularly where Temple Hall stood, the site of which was included afterward within the yard belonging to New Coll. Stables.'[23]

A court at St John's was sited in the north-east corner of the old Grove, where Loggan shows one of his rectangles, suggesting an unroofed building. It was first mentioned in the college account book (*Computus Annuus*) for 1623 and first used in the following year, when the college paid twenty-six shillings 'for finishing the Tennis Court and bowling alley'. A few years later, in 1639, the very large sum of £19 8s. 4d. was spent on '*Spheristeria*' (court and alley), and in 1641 there was a further expenditure of £2 4s. on 'the Ball Court'.[24]

It may be inferred from these sums that this was among the most luxurious of college courts, but it lasted for less than a century. In

College Ball Courts

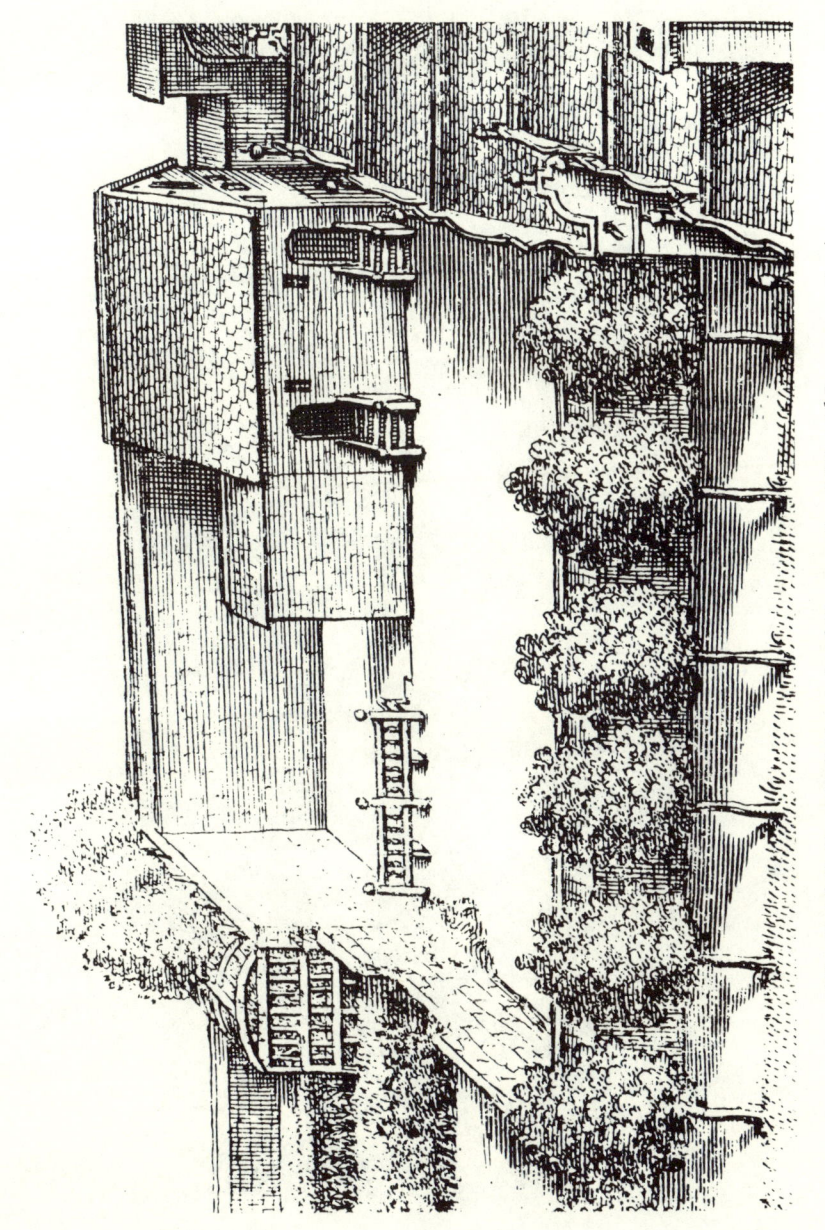

The Oriel College Ball Court (and Necessarium) (David Loggan, 1675)

Chapter 5

The Pembroke College Ball Court (David Loggan, 1675)

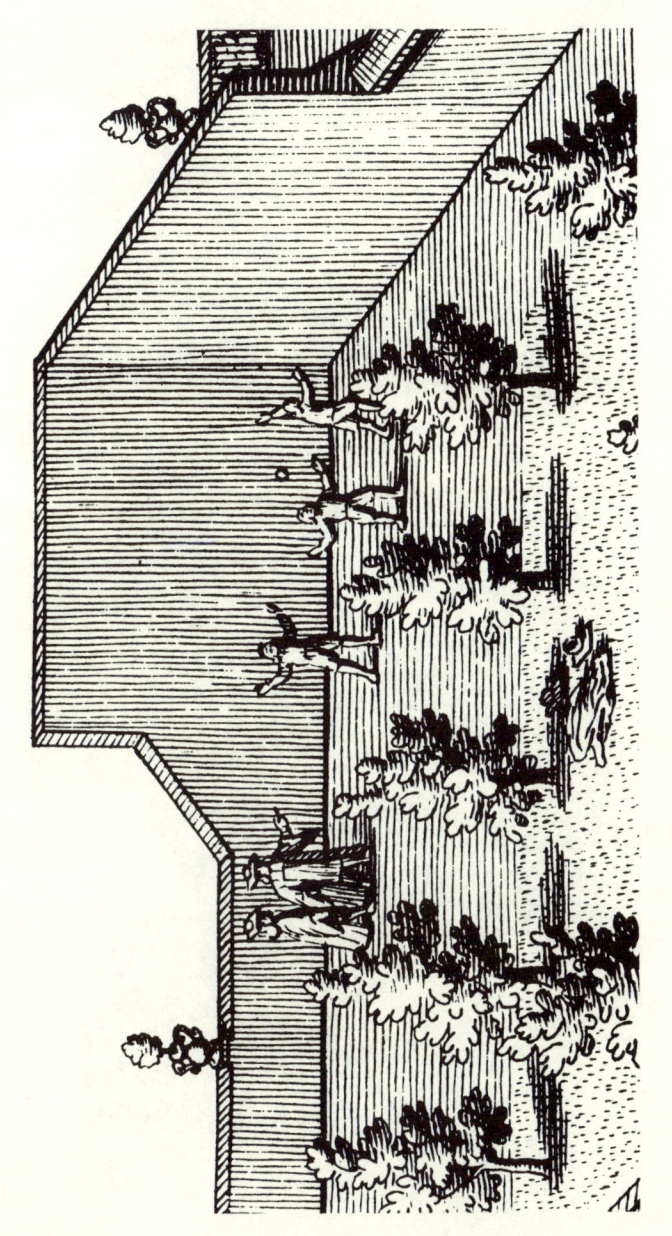

The Pembroke College Ball Court (Michael Burghers, 1700)

Chapter 5

The University College Ball Court (David Loggan, 1675)

1721 its disappearance was lamented by an old member on a return visit to the college. 'I missed the old Ball-Court where I have had many a game of Fifes when I was a young man,' wrote Nicholas Amhurst.[25] He noticed its absence when 'looking to my right hand' on entering the college through the back gate.

Amhurst had matriculated in 1706; so by that date, it appears, handball had ceased to be described as tennis. But whatever the game was called he was no better advertisement for it than Merton's Richard Holt had been. His time as an undergraduate had been curtailed when he was expelled from the university for libertinism and general misconduct. On his return, however, he was on good enough terms with one of the Fellows to be told the cause of the court's destruction. The President, 'having, some time ago, a mind for a *summer-house* in his garden to be built at the expense of the College, demolished it for the sake of the stones, which were to serve for a foundation to this new projected edifice; though it was pretended to be done to prevent the scholars from *lingering* away their time, and neglecting their studies'. But the Fellows refused to pay for the summer-house, 'and the stones were applied to another use'.[26]

Also at St John's, the space in front of the kitchen door at the end of the Hall Passage was at one time known as The Fives: a name which may have preserved the memory of the site of an earlier ball-play area. A new pavement of Headington rag stone was laid there in 1616/17.[27]

University College's court stood in what is now the south-east corner of the garden of the Master's Lodgings. As illustrated by Loggan, it was of much the same type as those at Christ Church and Oriel, having three full walls and a buttress forming a short length of a fourth.

The court at Hart Hall, like that at Queen's, is known only from a single mention by Anthony Wood, this time in the course of his researches into another, long vanished students' hall. Cat Hall, he wrote in the 1660s, 'stood where Hart Hall ball-court now is'.[28] This places it opposite the south-east corner of the schools quadrangle, a short distance from where the Smith Gate courts stood.

Hart Hall may not have been the only hall with a court. At Worcester College there is an oral tradition that a heightened section of the college's Walton Street wall, at the north-east corner of the Fellows Garden, formed part of a ball court constructed by one of its predecessors on the site: the Benedictine monks' Gloucester College or the post-Dissolution Gloucester Hall.

Neither Wood nor Loggan recognised the existence of the earlier, well-documented court at Lincoln, which, to judge from Loggan's view, appears to have been converted into a garden by his time. In this and other colleges the Fellows may have come to prefer peace and quiet to healthy but boisterous exercise within the college walls. The paucity of references and their often simple structure make it likely that some of these college ball courts did not enjoy a long life. Indeed, with a span of some two centuries at most, all were transient phenomena in relation to the longevity both of tennis and of the colleges themselves.

Clearly such scanty evidence paints an incomplete picture. It cannot be that some colleges had courts only in the sixteenth century and others only in the seventeenth. In most there was probably a succession of ball courts, becoming less rudimentary as time passed. Even if so, the picture is not an impressive one so far as the true game is concerned. The pattern was of plain, open walls with no indication of penthouses, tambour or grille. The contrast with Cambridge is striking. There, although the total number of college courts was fewer, there is sufficient evidence of frequent repairs and the erection of ever more sophisticated structures. There, when a ball court had to be pulled down, it is clear that some colleges – Corpus, St John's, Trinity – at once built other, more modern replacements on new sites within the college.

Yet at both universities almost every court within college precincts vanished in the course of the eighteenth century. (The sole survivor was at Pembroke College, Cambridge.) The space they occupied was needed for other new buildings, and it was a period when everywhere in the world tennis was suffering a gradual and then abrupt loss of favour.

In France the watershed was the Revolution. Already at a low ebb, the former national pastime finally lost all popularity – and its patrons their heads – in the aftermath of the historic oath taken (so inappropriately) in the tennis court at Versailles.

In England in 1797 *The Times* reported that the once fashionable game of tennis was very much upon the decline. Yet if *courte paume* seemed to be dying, according to a report in the *Sporting Magazine* in 1793 the outdoor game of *longue paume*, which required no walls or other facilities apart from rackets and balls, was very much alive. 'Field-tennis threatens ere long to bowl out cricket,' it went so far as to predict.[29]

To what extent this forerunner of lawn tennis was enjoyed by Oxford's citizens, dons and undergraduates in the fields surrounding the city can only be conjectured. But, despite the end of the era of college courts, excellent facilities for practising the authentic game of *courte paume* remained available to those who could afford it. Here, in the heart of the city, a tradition already at least three and a half centuries old was not broken.

CHAPTER 6

Courts, Inns and Theatres

IN 1760 the locally published *Companion to the Guide* boasted of 'three spacious and superb edifices, situated to the southward of the High Street, 100 feet long, by 30 in breadth, vulgarly called *Tennis Courts*, where *Exercise* is regularly performed both morning and afternoon'.[1]

These well-equipped public courts were the successors to those at Smith Gate and the sole survivors among possibly numerous ball courts which had flourished and faded in private back gardens and the courtyards of inns. Located in Blue Boar Lane, Oriel Street and Merton Street respectively, all three were leasehold properties kept by professional racket court keepers (in traditional parlance, *paumiers*), who were qualified to maintain them, make balls, string rackets and teach and mark the game. Their convenient situation within the area occupied by the university goes some way towards explaining why colleges did not choose to incur the expense of building proper tennis courts of their own.

Thomas Burnham, whose name deserves to be honoured as one of the most important in the history of Oxford tennis, kept all three courts in turn. Humbly born, he was in the service of Anthony Wood's family for some forty years from 1625. A man of outstanding ability, he became a superior and trusted servant. At the beginning of the Civil Wars, when pressure of business prevented Wood's father from his duty of training with the scholars and privileged men, his place was taken by Burnham, 'his next servant', who wore his master's helmet and back- and breast-piece and was armed with his pike and musket.[2]

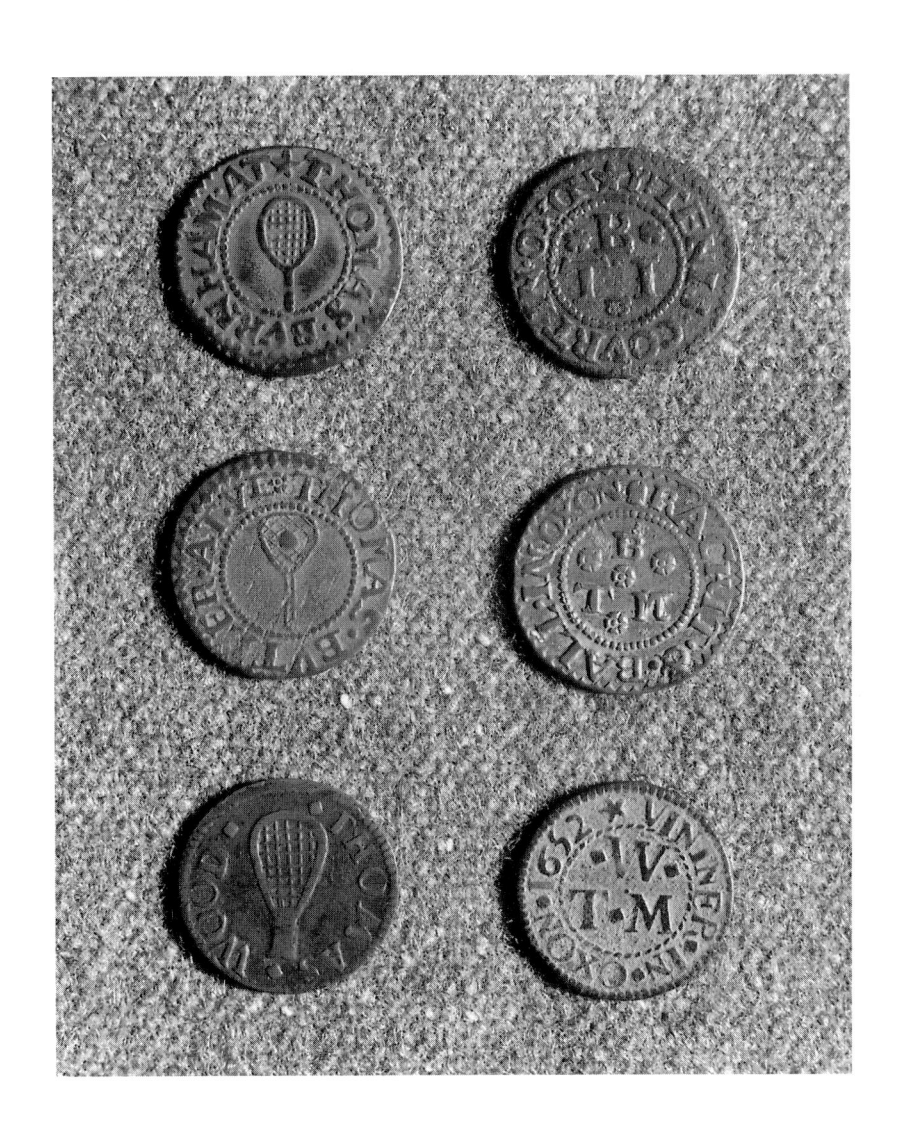

*Tradesmen's Tokens of
Oxford Tennis Court Keepers (17th Century)*

[facing page 56]

Extract from a Letter from the Visitor to the Fellows of Brasenose College (1608/9)

Second Letter from the Visitor to the Fellows of Brasenose College (1609)

*James Russell Gives a Lesson to the Prince of Wales,
the Future King Edward VII, on the Oriel Street Court (1859)*

The Wood family held the lease of the property on which the Merton Street court stood, and Burnham was granted a sub-lease of the court from 1647 until at least 1663, when he achieved independence by taking over the sub-lease of the Oriel Street court instead or as well. Seven years later he moved again, this time acquiring the lease of both the tennis court and the Unicorn Inn in Blue Boar Lane. Although, in conjunction with his tennis activities, he had held an ale-house licence since 1654, he chose to close the inn and rebuild the tennis court on a grander scale to make it the best in town.

Keeping a tennis court was a recognised trade, and Burnham became a freeman of the city in 1650, paying five pounds for the privilege. Respected in his dual role as *paumier* and publican, he qualified to become one of Oxford's leading citizens. Elected a bailiff in 1665 (when he was described as an innholder), he held that office for three years and remained a member of the City Council until at least 1670, when he was excused from wearing a gown on grounds of ill health.[3]

Burnham's death on 20 June 1676 was, accordingly, a noteworthy event. Anthony Wood recorded that on that day 'the great bell of Merton College rung out for Thomas Burnham of the Unicorn in St Aldate's parish'.[4] His will was sealed with a circular seal depicting a tennis racket flanked by his initials. In the inventory accompanying it, the lease of the Unicorn 'Rackett Court' was valued at the then considerable sum of £550 – clear evidence that keeping a tennis court in Oxford in the seventeenth century could be a lucrative business. The lease was inherited by his widow, who is listed in the city records for 1679 as 'Joane Burnham tenis court keeper', although doubtless she employed others to keep it for her.

At this period the royal mint had not yet begun to strike coinage in base metal. The demand for small-value coins had to be satisfied locally by tradesmen issuing redeemable tokens, usually worth a farthing. From Merton Street Burnham issued a token in the form of a small copper coin bearing an inscription which ran round the emblem of a racket and ball on one side and his initials on the other. When at Oriel Street, he issued another, also depicting a racket, his initials and a similar inscription: 'Thomas Burnham at ye Tenis Court in Oxon'.

As with the association between court and inn in Blue Boar Lane, so too in Oriel Street. That court lay behind the premises of the Salutation (later Crown) tavern, which stood on a site now numbered 104 and 105 High Street. Burnham's predecessor at the court, Thomas Wood or Woods, had also been the licensee of the Salutation and publicised the connection by issuing tokens with his name and a racket on one side and his initials and 'Vintner in Oxon 1651' on the other.

The connection was also advertised in the inn itself. At that time wine was carried from cask to table in dark-green bottles, and it became fashionable for these to be marked with the seals of taverns or individuals. A blob of hot glass was applied to the bottle and stamped with an appropriate emblem – a mermaid or a crown or a nobleman's coronet. Thomas Wood elected to have, under his initials, a representation of two tennis-players waving their rackets (in an unlikely manner) at a scattering of balls, eight in all. One of his long-necked sack bottles with this seal on the shoulder was found on the site of the Forestry Laboratory in Museum Road in 1906 and may be seen today in the Ashmolean Museum. Examples of Wood's and Burnham's tokens are in the museum's coin collection.

Wood became a freeman of the city in 1646 and died in 1663. He took over the Oriel Street court, the house beside it and the liquor licence for the inn from the widow of the previous owner, Richard Edwards (the 'Mr Edwards' of Charles I's time), who had died intestate. In 1652 he experienced a brush with the law when accused of selling wine without a licence. As further evidence of his versatility (and keenness to maximise the use of his court), he was also in business as a dancing master.

This Thomas Wood needs to be distinguished both from Thomas Wood the stonemason or 'stone cutter' at Smith Gate and from the Thomas Wood who was Anthony Wood's father and held the lease of the Merton Street court. Anthony Wood identifies him as the son of a servant in his father's family; hence possibly the adoption of the name.[5] However that may be, it is a curious and confusing fact that during the seventeenth century public tennis courts in Oxford were kept by three different individuals with the same name.

There was, too, a preponderance of Thomases. After Thomas Wood and Thomas Burnham at Oriel Street came Thomas Butler. He was apprenticed to Thomas Burnham for eight years from March 1660 and on completion of his apprenticeship was admitted to the freedom of the city in August 1668. Two years later he moved to a court of his own, taking the lease of the remaining Smith Gate court and holding it until its closure in 1690. There he issued tokens inscribed 'Thomas Butler at Rackit & Ball in Oxford'. (One is in the Ashmolean with Wood's and Burnham's.) Whether or not he also doubled as an alehouse keeper is not certain, but one Hudson, his predecessor at the Smith Gate court, was the licensee of an alehouse in the parish of St Peter-in-the-East, where the court was situated.[6]

As commercial enterprises and substantial buildings in the centre of town, all these tennis courts were readily available for hire and in habitual use for other activities besides the game itself.

They served as gymnasia and suitable venues for boxing and wrestling matches; as halls for dances and dancing classes; and for concerts, acrobatic displays and spectacles of all kinds. One example in the last category is known from an entry in the diary of Thomas Crosfield of Queen's, dated July 1635, which mentions among current entertainments 'dansing on ye rope at ye racket Court, by the blewbore'.[7]

The most common secondary use was for the staging of plays. When courts were roofed they became more attractive venues for actors and audiences than the courtyards of inns exposed to the vagaries of the weather. It did not take Thomas Burnham's rebuilt court in Blue Boar Lane long to attract theatrical – and sometimes unruly – custom. When the tragedy of *Cambises, King of Persia* was performed there in the summer of 1671,[8] the following proclamation was posted in the streets:

> By Order from Mr Vice-Chancellor
> Whereas complaint has been brought to Me of several disorders committed in and about the New Tenis-Court, where His Royall Highness the Duke of York's Servants now Act; These are to require all Persons whatsoever, not to give them any disturbance, during the time assigned them for their stay in the University, upon pain of being proceeded against as disturbers of the Publick Peace, and the good Orders and Discipline of this place.
>
> P. Mews, Vice-Canc.
July 10, 1671[9]

In France, before the age of purpose-built theatres, Molière's troupe of players regularly performed in tennis courts when on tour, and London companies enjoyed the same facilities in Oxford. In 1703, for instance, Thomas Betterton, the brightest star of the day, arrived with his company to perform in one of the courts. They came from a theatre which was itself a converted tennis court, visited by Pepys after its opening following the Restoration: 'Mr Shepley and I to the new play-house near Lincoln's-Inn-Fields, (which was formerly Gibbon's tennis-court)...'[10] At a later date a similar transformation was to take place in Oxford.

The use of tennis courts as theatres continued throughout the eighteenth century, but irregularly in Oxford until the end of the century when a Georgian impresario named Henry Thornton received permission to stage plays annually during the long vacation. He then formed Oxford's first professional theatrical company. This performed in the Merton Street court for seven years from 1799, and such was its popularity that on one occasion seven hundred people had to be turned away. The title of the play performed in August 1799, Oliver Goldsmith's *She Stoops to Conquer*, was singularly apt: in tennis stooping to conquer is a phrase signifying the approved method of stroke play (with the head of the racket held higher than the wrist while the player adopts the so-called commode position).

For theatrical performances a temporary stage was erected against the main wall, fronted by a proscenium arch and backed by the traditional green curtain. Gentry were accommodated on chairs in the galleries; common folk sat on benches on the floor of the court. In 1807 the company moved to the 'more commodious' court in Blue Boar Lane.[11] There, when His Majesty's Servants from the Theatre Royal Windsor had presented readings from 'Colman's Drama of *The Mountaineer*' in 1802, separate entrances were specified: to the upper gallery from the lane itself; to the boxes and pit through the Bull Inn in St Aldate's.

As the various uses to which the Oxford courts have been put bear witness, tennis-court buildings can be adapted for other purposes without difficulty and are therefore not lightly destroyed, even when no longer required for the purpose for which they were originally erected. Since the high tide of enthusiasm for the game receded, courts have been left stranded but still standing, converted into gymnasia, art galleries, chapels or warehouses – even homes for battery hens – in cities as far afield as Dublin, Paris, Stockholm, Prague, St Petersburg and Chicago, and at country houses as near as Heythrop House in Oxfordshire. Yet in Oxford itself no trace remains of the Smith Gate courts which, in one case, provided a public service for nearly two hundred years (c. 1500–1690), nor of Thomas Burnham's fine building in Blue Boar Lane which, with its predecessor, spanned an even longer period.

CHAPTER 7

The Blue Boar Courts

THE FIRST court in what was to become Blue Boar Lane stood in the back yard of an inn named The Racket. This suggests either that the two were built at the same time as a joint enterprise or that an established alehouse changed its name to advertise a new attraction when the legal prohibitions against tennis lost their force.

The earliest surviving mention occurs at a relevant date: towards the end of Henry VIII's reign. In the year 27 Henry VIII (1535/36) a 30-year lease of the property, lying between tenements occupied by a brewer to the north and a barber to the south, was granted by Christ Church, the freeholder, to Robert Benbowe. The rent was 26s. 8d. per annum.[1] A further reference to a 'Tennes Court' among the property of Cardinal College occurs in 1546. Thereafter the existence of a court in active use is recorded at intervals for almost three centuries.

In 1555, when the lease passed to John Vawse, the property was described as having the New Lane on the north, and the rent was halved to 13s. 4d. Evidently what was later called Bear Lane, and later still Blue Boar Lane, had been driven through the site to make a new exit from Fish Street (now St Aldate's). From that time inn and court became situated on a corner site on the south side of this lane at its junction with the main road to Folly Bridge, with the college timber yard to the east.

In 1587 the property was demised to John Lant (Launt or Lante), a Student, that is a Fellow, of Christ Church and son to Bartholomew Lant, licensee of one of the Smith Gate courts. Eight years later he was to build the court in Merton Street.

The tenancy of a Student of the college illustrates the need to identify and distinguish between leaseholders who were gentlemen with an interest in tennis for enjoyment or investment and professional players with the status of tradesmen whose livelihood came from keeping the courts for themselves. Sometimes the one held the lease, the other a sub-lease. Both employed assistants. Leases, moreover, were sometimes assignable and usually inheritable, so that they not infrequently (as after the deaths of Richard Edwards, Thomas Burnham and others) fell into the hands of widows whose sole interest in a tennis court would lie in its value and the income it produced. In the case of Lant *père et fils* it can only be surmised whether they were gentlemanly tennis buffs, as seems likely, or merely shrewd businessmen who exploited a rising demand and never themselves put hand to ball or racket.

At some date prior to 1629, when the lease passed to William Bust, The Racket inn had been renamed The Sign of the Unicorn. The reason is unknown, but tennis play was not affected. John Hemsley took over the lease in 1645, and it was renewed in his name in 1666. Bust and Hemsley were, it seems, professionals.

There is a curious reference to 'Hensland's racquet court' in the city records concerning an incident relating to the municipal water supply. In April 1656 a pipe which carried water from the Carfax Conduit and ran under the court began to leak. With 'the water coming up into his court' it was reported that the keeper 'hath cut the pipe': apparently with a fine disregard for the consequences elsewhere.[2]

The result of Thomas Burnham's acquisition of the lease and rebuilding of the court in 1670 is recorded in an entry in Christ Church's *Book of Evidences* made fourteen years later: 'Since the last renewing, this Tenement is not used as an Inne, but a fair and stately Racket Court is built, covered over head, which it was not before.' What had been replaced was 'an Inne with a Backside & stables thereto belonging, and a fair Racket Court'. Loggan's view of the city in 1675 shows a building with six windows, parallel to and abutting on the lane. No longer relegated to a rear courtyard, it had been moved forward to occupy the site of the inn's frontage.

In the eighteenth and nineteenth centuries the international reputation of French *paumiers* stood as high as that of French chefs. The court at Catherine the Great's military academy in St Petersburg, for example, was staffed by a succession of Frenchmen. Oxford's French *paumier* was named David Pillett or, more plausibly, Pillet. In 1760 a news item in *Jackson's Oxford Journal* referred to a house for sale in Blue Boar Lane occupied by Pillet;[3] another in 1763 referred to 'Pillet's Tennis Court';[4] and another two years later to the estate of the late Mr David Pillett (executor Susanna Pillett, widow) at the Tennis Court, Blue Boar Lane.[5] The better-known Thomas Pillet subsequently kept the court in Oriel Street.

The last mention of the Blue Boar court as a going concern is of a new dressing room in 1829. The end came three years later. In March 1832 an estimate was received 'for converting the Racket Court into Stable Offices'; and in November an account for £1266 17s. 5d. was rendered to the Dean and Chapter for turning the court into stables and coach houses.[6]

The sad demise of this fair and stately court may have been due as much to declining custom as to the college's need for improved stabling. Tennis had become too costly for most pockets, and the demand in Oxford was by this date insufficient to maintain three well-appointed and adequately staffed courts.

'Had we no expensive amusements? Yes, one very expensive one, especially for a beginner, tennis,' wrote a memoirist of his time at Magdalen Hall in the 1830s. 'When you first begin, the game is so short that you lose it in four or five strokes, which take about five minutes; and, as games are played in sets of six games, and each set cost seven shillings, our early tennis certainly cost fourteen shillings an hour, which, as Oxford amusements went, was rather dear.'[7]

CHAPTER 8

The Oriel Street Courts

THE ORIGINAL Oriel Street tennis court is first mentioned in a lease of 1572. It was built in the garden of one or more houses standing on the site of Agas Hall in what was then St Mary Hall Lane. The land, which lay to the rear of the present 104 and 105 High Street, formerly belonged to the Chantry of St Thomas in the university church of St Mary the Virgin.[1]

Today the building occupies a central position within Oriel College's 'Island Site', a block bounded by High Street, Oriel Street, Oriel Square and King Edward Street. The whole area came into the college's possession piecemeal: in the case of the tennis court a small portion of the southern end towards the close of the seventeenth century; the remainder not until 1878 when the building had ceased to be used for tennis.[2]

The 1572 lease was to Henry Mylward, the haberdasher who had obtained a licence for a tennis court from the Crown in 1555. It identifies the site as 'now a tennis playe'. The 'now' may signify 'new', but it could just as well mean that the court had been built some years earlier, that is, since the date of a previous lease. The haberdasher's family was still in possession in 1608, when the property was described as the tennis-play of Alice Milward, widow. The original building was probably an open wooden structure, but by 1600 it was roofed.

Excavation by the Oxford Archaeological Unit in 1990 revealed a rebuilding in stone in the late 1630s: the oak timber used was found to have been felled in 1637. The chase lines were then marked by narrow strips of black shale-like stone inserted between the main stone slabs paving the floor. The numbers were painted on the wall, as is the present custom.[3]

This new building was oriented almost due north–south. Its internal measurements were 94 feet in length and 29 in width; but, allowing for the galleries, the playing area at ground level would have been appreciably smaller. The archaeological evidence also revealed that the court had had to be repeatedly re-floored in later times owing to subsidence, and that it was re-roofed with Scandinavian pine between 1776 and 1786.[4]

This court antedated Thomas Burnham's in Blue Boar Lane and was thus the most modern in Oxford in the 1640s. That would explain why Charles I and Prince Rupert chose to play here in preference to the courts in Merton Street and Blue Boar Lane, even though the latter lay closer to the royal quarters in Christ Church. (During the siege those two may well have been commandeered for use as armouries or for storing provisions.)

In 1636 the property, including the tavern on the High Street frontage, passed to Richard Edwards, a surgeon. He lived on the premises in St Mary Hall Lane, occupying, in Anthony Wood's words, 'Edwards his house at the racket court'.[5] In 1651 the lease was in the name of his widow, Katherine. In 1672 it passed to Francis Nash Gregory DD, of Hambledon, Bucks, and further leases were granted to his widow, Mary, in 1711 and 1725.[6] It was during this period that sub-leases of the court, together with the tavern licences, were held by Thomas Wood, Thomas Burnham, Thomas Butler and their successors as keepers.

Parry, the keeper in the 1760s, was in the busness of selling balls, not only to those who patronised his court but also to other professionals at a trade discount. This was a service which he advertised from time to time in the local press. In an advertisement in 1765, for example, he announced:

E. Parry at the Tennis Court in St Mary Hall Lane, Oxford, Makes and Sells, Wholesale and Retail, the very best Tennis and Fives Balls of all Sizes; and which are allowed by Gentlemen to exceed all that they have bought elsewhere. He also makes Cricket Balls; and an allowance will be made to those who sell them again. The Tennis Balls, uncovered at One Guinea per Gross; and two Guineas covered.[7]

An Uncovered Ball

The phrase 'of all sizes' in Parry's advertisement provides evidence that, in the course of the game's development from handball to increasingly sophisticated racket play, convention and practice in the eighteenth century were still sufficiently fluid for players to choose their own size of ball in accordance with the type of game preferred.

The eight balls found in 1985 lodged behind the collar of the end truss at the screens of the hall in Wadham consist of strips of coarse woollen or cotton fabric held in shape, much like the modern ball, by a network of knotted string. Some are covered in fine white leather; others uncovered. Their sizes vary between 4¼ and 6½ inches in circumference. They are thought to date from the seventeenth century.[8] Pepys, who was 'cut for the stone' at that time, used to display that grisly object as a trophy after his operation and claim that it was as big as a tennis ball. Weighing two ounces, it would have been the size of a modern fives ball.[9]

The enterprising Mr Parry was in the entertainment business too. Between 1762 and 1765 the anniversary of George III's birthday in June was celebrated with his firework display at the Horse and Jockey inn near Folly Bridge. Public rejoicing in Oxford at news of the birth of an heir to the throne (the future George IV) was similarly marked by a display of Mr Parry's fireworks.

His successor at the tennis court was yet another Thomas. He was Thomas Pillet, presumably a son of David Pillett, the anglicised Frenchman who had kept the Blue Boar court. This Thomas was a former dragoon in the French king's service, and his temperament and military experience in France do not seem to have fitted him for a tranquil life in Oxford, for he was soon crossing swords with the authorities. He was accused of extortion: a charge which he at first bragged about and then vehemently denied. The denial was made in a fine show of legal bravado in a notice published in *Jackson's Oxford Journal* during the season of good will, 1769:

> Whereas Richard Lloyd, a Writer in the Town Clerk's Office, did, on Wednesday the 29th Day of November, 1769, scandalously and maliciously report, with intent to injure and prejudice me, Thomas Pillet, Keeper of the Tennis Court

in St-Mary-Hall-Lane in Oxford, that I had at divers Times, extorted Money from different Gentlemen of the University of Oxford, in the said Court: Which Report I am ready to prove, under the Hands of most (if not all) the Gentlemen of this University who have, ever since I have kept the said Court, used the same, to be false: Now I the said Thomas Pillet, in this publick manner, call upon the said Richard Lloyd, to make appear (if he possibly can) what he has maliciously asserted, otherwise he may depend upon being treated according to his Deserts.[10]

Lloyd proved by no means intimidated by this challenge and scarcely veiled threat. His response appeared in the same newspaper the following week. It reminded Pillet that he had boasted of defrauding undergraduates. It asserted for good measure that he got drunk and swore at people. It ended by declaring Lloyd's intention of taking the matter to court.[11] What happened next is, unfortunately, not known.

Tall and muscular, Pillet was an accomplished tennis-player. His stroke play was heavy, and his strategy was to occupy the middle of the court and attack the ball fiercely on the volley. But brilliance on court was marred by his quarrelsome nature, a violent temper and behaviour which shocked opponents and spectators. This led to his downfall despite a profound knowledge of the game, which he would have learned from his father from childhood and which qualified him to become an excellent teacher. He might, too, have earned a good living from making rackets: his, alone in England, were acknowledged to be as good as any made in France.

Instead, he threw up his job in Oxford to lead a nomadic existence, moving restlessly from court to court in England, France and beyond, paying his way by playing challenge matches at cramped odds. Wielding instead of a racket his famous *sabre de bois*, a mace three feet long and no more than four inches wide, he could beat even the most skilled of amateurs: doubtless to their great surprise and cost. Reputed to be one of the two best English players during the latter part of the eighteenth century, he was denied the status of champion by his own stormy disposition. He was reduced instead to achieving a niche in tennis's hall of fame as an itinerant genius – perhaps launched on that career by the town clerk's office in Oxford.[12]

Meanwhile proprietorship of the Oriel Street court had passed from the Gregorys to Mabbots or Mabbotts: to Gilbert Mabbot in 1753 and William Mabbott in 1781. William lived in Reading, and in 1798 the court and adjoining house were in the occupation of John Hardaway, the then keeper of the court. Hardaway died in 1812, and in the following year the Mabbott family sold the property to his children, Anne, Sophia and Thomas.[13]

Thomas had been apprenticed to his father, 'racket and ball maker', for seven years from 1 November 1793, but revenue from hire of the court and supplying rackets and balls must have been too small to furnish both of them with a living: at the time of the sale this new Oriel Street Thomas was described as a 'dealer in corn'. But he then assumed management of the court, at least as a part-time occupation, being later identified as 'corn dealer and tennis court keeper'.[14]

His tennis business did not prosper: this was a period when the game was growing more expensive and less popular. In 1835 he was forced to mortgage the court as security for a £100 debt, and to do so again shortly afterwards in respect of two further charges. In 1838 he retired, granting a four-year lease at £50 a year jointly to his son, Thomas Hardaway the younger, and James Russell.

Russell was the famous Duck-legged Jem or Duck-Leg Jim, the

paumier who kept what came to be known as Russell's court for the next twenty years, acquiring more of a reputation as a character than a player. A betting man, a boozer and a joker, he was evidently the best of company. His idea of cramped odds was to play with a boot jack or a soda-water or ginger-beer bottle on the end of a wooden stick.

His partnership with the younger Thomas Hardaway ran quickly into debt and was dissolved after only eighteen months. It was not disputed that during that time 'the management and conduct of the said business have devolved almost entirely upon James Russell', who proceeded to buy out his sleeping partner. He relieved Hardaway of responsibility for his half of the debts, paid him £53 and became the sole proprietor.[15]

Assisted by a marker named Foulkes, he struggled on through a tangle of growing debts and further mortgages until 1857 when the court closed. A combination of hard times, poor management and competition from a superior establishment in Merton Street had brought it to death's door.

The building then began a new, but short-lived, existence as a grandly named theatre, approachable either from 6 Oriel Street (for the stalls and pit) or down a narrow passage from High Street (for the gallery). In August 1857 an advertisement announced a performance at the Theatre Royal, Oriel Street, by permission of the Reverend the Vice-Chancellor and the Right Worshipful the Mayor. A double bill to suit all tastes featured Shakespeare's *Tragedy of Othello* followed by a farce of local interest entitled *Did you ever send your wife to Nuneham?* Singing and Dancing every evening were promised, and there were Hippodrama nights, when thespian horses performed.

Yet even this wide range of attractions proved insufficient to keep the theatre in business, and the next step was down market to billiards. For a short time this was combined with a return to tennis, the tables presumably being removed at certain hours when the building was temporarily restored to its proper use. During this twilight period before its permanent closure Russell and the court enjoyed one last burst of glory.

Apart from Frederick, Prince of Wales, who is alleged to have died from it, the House of Hanover displayed none of royalty's historic zeal for playing ball games. But royal patronage of tennis was revived when the future Edward VII came up to Oxford in October 1859, a month before his eighteenth birthday, and Duck-legged Jem was selected to be his tennis tutor. A surviving print on deckle-edged cream board, surmounted by the prince's crest, pictures the future king as an undergraduate 'taking his first lesson in Tennis' (in the words of the caption) 'under the instruction of Mr James Russell (Old Jim), at the Old Tennis Court, Oriel Street, Oxford'. The print is signed by Russell and may have been sold by him as a souvenir.

After the court had been made over wholly to billiards, Russell retired to Summertown ('a village near Oxford') where he died in June 1868, aged 55, after a long illness, leaving a widow and eight (out of eleven) surviving children. In his will he was described as 'late tennis court keeper' with the rueful subsequent amendment: 'but now Billiard Table Keeper'.

Under the terms of his will all Russell's property went to his wife, Jane, for life. As a joint executor with her and as trustee for the children after his death he named his rival tennis professional, 'my friend Thomas William Sabin of Merton Street'. But, although Russell had become a man of property (in both Oxford and Summertown), he died as he had lived: in debt. Within twelve months his widow was forced to take out more mortgages, and in the following year Sabin shed his responsibilities with a formal disclaimer and renunciation of his duties as executor and trustee, swearing that he had never acted.

Russell's heirs then sold all his property to a solicitor in Brighton, named Somers Clarke, for £1650. A Sussex lawyer seems an unlikely purchaser, but Clarke may well have been acting on behalf of, or in partnership with, Sabin's successor at Merton Street, Edmund Tompkins. Two of Tompkins's brothers were tennis and rackets court keepers in Brighton, and Edmund himself later went to live there in retirement.

In 1876 Tompkins bought the court – now four billiard rooms – from Clarke for £1550; although Clarke continued to hold a mortgage on the property. Then, only two years later, they sold it, together with an adjoining site 'where once was a house built by Sophia Hardaway', to Oriel College for £1800.

If Tompkins had been attempting to revive tennis in Oriel Street he had failed, and it was the last attempt to be made. The years of the court's decline were summed up in a 'Declaration by Edmund Tompkins of the Willows, Upper Heyford in the County of Oxford, Tennis Court Proprietor', dated 27 March 1878. In this he declared that he was fifty-one years old and had known the billiard rooms, formerly a tennis court, for thirty years; and that what was originally a tennis court had become 'racquet and billiard rooms' and then billiard rooms only.

Leases to the Gregory and Mabbott families had recognised the college's ownership of a small part of the land. In 1821 this had been leased to the Hardaways for seven years at £4 a year. In 1853 it was referred to as a 'piece or parcel of ground, whereon the South end or portion of a certain Tennis Court now stands, lying behind or on the Western part or side of a certain messuage belonging to the college and now in the occupation of the said James Russell'. This messuage was probably 13 Oriel Street.

For many years the college put the building to use as lecture rooms. During the Second World War it was called into service as a safe repository housing 40,000 books.[16] Later it served as a bicycle store and as a recreation area for table tennis. The unusually small playing area and lack of demand for a second Oxford court militated against any endeavour to bring it back into use as a tennis court.

Today the stone walls with their high windows on either side still stand between Oriel Street and King Edward Street proclaiming their original purpose, but nothing of the interior of the court remains, not even the tambour. The site now lies within the Oriel College precincts, connected to the main college buildings by a tunnel under Oriel Street. As the centrepiece of some recent extensive refurbishment and redevelopment within the Island Site, its conversion to twenty-two student rooms above ground level was completed in 1993, with a lecture hall and common rooms below to follow. In this new guise the former playground of kings was formally opened by the Prime Minister, John Major, in the autumn of that year.

CHAPTER 9

The First Merton Street Court

AFTER the disappearance of all the college ball courts, the demolition of the court in Blue Boar Lane and the end of tennis in Oriel Street, the court situated on the north side of Merton Street became the only active court in Oxford. Since the middle of the nineteenth century it has been 'the Oxford court'.

The original building on this site makes its first recorded appearance in a lease dated 6 October 1595, when Postmasters Hall was demised by Merton College to John Lante, MA (Oxon), 'with the backside and garden plot to same belonging and a tennise court of late built and erected thereon by the said John Lante'.[1] 'Late built' in October 1595 is the only clue to the precise date of completion, but in the absence of any mention in a previous lease it seems likely to have been earlier the same year.

This was the same Lante (Lant, Lantt or Launt) who was a Student of Christ Church and held the lease of the Blue Boar court from that college. No details of what he built behind Postmasters Hall have survived, but the court was almost certainly roofed when first erected. Loggan's view in the next century shows a tall, gabled building, oriented east-west, with blank lower walls and windows under the eaves, much resembling the exterior of a modern court.

The duration of the lease was for forty years initially, but on 20 March 1610 it was assigned to Thomas Wood, BA (Oxon), on the same terms, again for forty years, and with the phrase describing the tennis court as 'of late built and erected thereon' left unchanged in the Merton College Register of Leases.[2] The whole property –

house, court and garden – was destined to stay in the hands of the Wood family as leaseholders until 1754.

This Thomas Wood was the father of the antiquarian Anthony. For the resident proprietor of an Oxford tennis court, his qualifications were impeccable. His son described him as 'tall & bigge', 'bred a scholare' and 'active in manlie sports'.[3] Born in 1580, he took his first degree at Corpus, followed by a BCL at Broadgates Hall (an institution later absorbed into Pembroke College). Remaining in Oxford, he matured into a sufficiently important and prosperous local businessman and property-owner to be offered a knighthood when James I was bestowing honours wholesale as a means of fund-raising. Wood, however, declined the title, probably reckoning that paying the fine for refusal (levied on those with clear incomes of more than £40 per annum) was the less expensive option.

Like Lante's, Wood's first lease did not run its full term, but it was renewed for another forty years from 12 October 1626, when the property was said to include 'Two tennise courts heeretofore or now lately built and erected thereon'.[4] Repetition of this phrase continued unaltered in subsequent leases, but it is not supported by any other evidence for the existence of a second court. All references in the writings of Anthony Wood, who was born in Postmasters Hall and lived there throughout his life (1632–95), are to one court only, and it is hard to believe that the garden plot could have accommodated a second. The only plausible explanations are the routine clerical copying of an error, perhaps originating in an aborted project, or the misleading designation of an outdoor practice area as a second court.

The latter could have been located for a short period in the narrow space lying between the north wall of the court and the south wall of University College. In the nineteenth century two fives courts were built end-on in this space, but for most of the seventeenth it was occupied by a 'little house in his backside' built by Thomas Wood in 1639 or 1640 as accommodation for the keeper of the court, his servant Thomas Burnham.[5] In 1642, when Oxford became the royalist capital during the Civil Wars, Wood and his family were forced to surrender Postmasters Hall to the Master of the Rolls and live in this little house themselves.

Wood died in 1643, and four years later the family granted Burnham a sub-lease on the court in his own right. This ran until 1670 and may have been retained by him during its last seven years, when he also held the sub-lease of the Oriel Street court. The leasehold interest in the whole Merton Street property was inherited by Wood's widow, Mary, to whom it was assigned in a new lease dated 18 April 1651.[6] Thirteen years later, when she too had died, the lease was renewed in the names of three of the sons – Robert, Christopher and Anthony – jointly.[7]

Although the rent to the college for the entire property amounted to no more than £6 2s. (unchanged in the course of two centuries), Anthony Wood's one-third share of the rent paid by the sub-lessee of the court was £8 6s. 8d. half-yearly. From this, £1 was deducted for his share of reserved rent payable to the college, leaving him with a net annual income from the court of £14 13s. 4d. But this, as he was at pains to record, was further reduced by liability for a share of repair and maintenance costs, for which the tenants were responsible.[8]

The chore of management was undertaken by Robert, the eldest of the brothers, while Christopher looked after other family properties and Anthony, a freeloading bachelor in Robert's household, immersed himself in scholarship and gossip and contributed little except some bad-tempered grumbling.

In February 1671, for example, Anthony wrote in his diary:

'received but £5 of monsier for the racket court (although should have had £7) because (as he pretends) that I forgave it'.[9] 'Monsier' was his sarcastic nickname for Robert. Another entry, dated September 1673, relates to court maintenance: 'Memorandum, that this long vacation my brother Robert paved the tennis court [costing] him about £11, of which I promised to pay £3 13s. towards it for my share.'[10]

Further leases were granted to the brothers in 1678, 1685 and 1692, Anthony's name being omitted from the first two but restored in the last. When he died, a bachelor to the end, he bequeathed his share of the houses, garden and tennis court to the by then dead Robert's daughters, Anne and Frances.

The property continued to pass to Wood descendants through new leases in 1712, 1726 and 1740, but from 1712 they were no longer resident in the city. The leaseholders from that date were Dr Thomas Wood, Rector of Hardwick (where, coincidentally, two tennis courts were built at a later date), and Robert Wood of Cumnor, a 'gent.' In 1726 the lease was granted to Dr Wood's widow, Joan Wood of London, and in 1740 to William Wood, a 'Haberdasher of Small Wares', who was also a Londoner.[11]

In 1754 the leaseholder was once more an Oxford citizen, but no longer from a university family. He was 'Francis Cobb, of the Parish of St John's in the City of Oxford, Cook'.[12] Whether his interest was in Postmasters Hall or the tennis court, it is impossible to determine, but it seems that at this period the lease was no more than an investment, with separate sub-tenants occupying Postmasters Hall and managing the court. In 1777 it passed to two non-resident spinsters: Anne Ellis of Cornhill, London and Mary Ellis of Leytonstone, Essex. In drawing up the terms of the leases throughout this entire period the college continued to alter nothing except the names of the lessees. It was still specifying two tennis courts and, in a pre-inflationary age, the annual rent remained at £6 2s.[13]

After two hundred years of use the court was rebuilt on the same site in 1798 or thereabouts. It then assumed the form which it retains to this day. This is notable for a number of peculiarities, some of which may have been inherited from the earlier building. Although larger than Oriel Street's, the dimensions of the playing area are smaller than the norm: approximately one yard shorter in length and two feet narrower in width (93 feet as against 96 and a little under 30 as against 32). The floor is fast but the walls are dead, so that it is a court which favours volleying. The penthouses are several inches lower than in other courts; which is a significant aid to the railroad service. The angle between the main wall and the tambour is exceptionally obtuse; which takes the uninitiated by surprise.

Variety between courts forms one of the challenges of tennis, and in this respect the special features of the Oxford court offer more than most.

CHAPTER 10

A Dynasty of Champions

THE LONGEVITY of the Wood family as tennis-court proprietors in Merton Street was matched by the record of the Tompkins family as professionals. Apart from one interregnum, the management and teaching of tennis on this court rested, from the middle of the eighteenth century until almost the middle of the twentieth, with this one Oxfordshire family. Successive generations took over the Merton Street lease and displayed a dazzling talent as exponents of the game.

They were tradesmen of yeoman stock, recorded first as small land-owners in the village of Waterperry, near Wheatley.[1] Robert and John were prosperous bakers in Forest Hill, and George and his son William kept a well-known grocer's shop in Oxford, at first in Cornmarket and then at Butter Bench near the Carfax Conduit. In retirement in 1763 George fell and broke a leg 'at Blue Boar',[2] perhaps paying the penalty for too much enthusiasm for an energetic ball game in old age. His son was highly enough regarded to be elected a bailiff of the city. The black sheep of the Tompkins family was Thomas, who was transported for seven years for stealing peas and beans.[3]

The tennis-playing branch of the family favoured the Christian name Edmund to such an extent that they have had to be distinguished by numbers like the kings they were. Edmund the First ('Tompkins of Waterperry') became keeper of the Merton Street court in 1758. Nothing else is known about his career, but in view of his renown as a player at the time of his tragically early death five years later he must have been employed in one or other of the courts from a much earlier date. His death was reported in these words:

> Last Sunday night Mr Edmund Tompkins, Master of one of the Racquet Courts in this city, and himself esteemed the best tennis player in England, was unhappily drowned in the Isis at Iffley Mill; whereby a widow and several children are left unprovided for; and whilst his more intimate Acquaintance lament him as a sincere and social friend, his Loss will be no less regretted by many of the Nobility and Gentry as a Man of the strictest integrity.[4]

This 'melancholy Accident' occurred in the course of an evening Pleasure Party on the river, when a swift current carried a boatload of merry-makers towards one of the sluices. Tompkins was among those who jumped from the boat, only to be lost in the water despite being a strong swimmer. When his body was recovered the next morning, it was discovered that he had suffered a blow on the head.

At Merton Street he was succeeded by his son, Edmund the Second, who, when he found the game not sufficiently well supported in Oxford, migrated to London to manage a court in Windmill Street. While there he played what was described as 'a great match' in the nearby James Street court against Mlle. Bunel, a leading French woman player of the day (who, when dressed in her court attire, was unkindly said to resemble a scarecrow). She was reported to have beaten him by two sets to one, but at what odds we do not know.[5]

Although absent, 'Edmund of Windmill Street' retained the Merton Street lease until his death. It was then inherited by his son, Edmund the Third, who had been born in Oxford (in 1802) and returned from London to take charge.

This Edmund was commonly known as Peter to distinguish him from his father. Like his grandfather, he was of championship class. Like his father, he was to become attracted by better opportunities and richer prospects away from Oxford, where the appeal of the game was diminished by its expense, although this was a period of general recovery from the doldrums of the eighteenth century. New courts were beginning to be opened elsewhere in England, and in 1836 a riding school in Brighton was converted into a tennis court. Peter accepted an invitation to manage it, graduating in due course to lessee and part-proprietor and handing on his interest in the court to his son John.

Although not strong enough to compete on level terms against the French champion, Edmond Barre, the celebrated Parisian *paumier* dubbed the 'greatest of all great players', Oxford-born Peter was recognised as the best English player of his day. A famous match between the two was played at Lord's in 1839, when Peter emerged victorious after a severe struggle, but only against an opponent conceding half thirty and a bisque. Barre held the World Championship for a record thirty-three years, taking it from one Oxford man in 1829 and ceding it to another in 1862.

Peter returned to Oxford in 1841 to play a series of money-making exhibition matches with the keepers of the two remaining courts: Thomas Sabin of Merton Street and James Russell (Duck-legged Jem) of Oriel Street. Sabin, who had taken over Peter's lease when he left for Brighton, was known as 'a civil and respectable man',[6] but to draw the crowds he was later to make history in Merton Street by playing a match on horseback.

The fourth player in the exhibition doubles matches in 1841 was W. J. Cox, the scion of another famous Oxford tennis dynasty. Cox's father, Philip Cox the elder, had been born in Oxford in 1779. He began his tennis career as a marker there, but soon moved to London, where he quickly won fame and fortune at the James Street court, which was then regarded as the headquarters of tennis in England. Under the nickname of 'Old Cox', to distinguish him from his three sons, all of whom followed in his footsteps as tennis professionals, he achieved a reputation as high as any of the Tompkins family. Acclaimed as one of the best players who ever lived, he was recognised as World Champion for ten years from 1819, until defeated by Barre.

A very similar career and success was enjoyed by Peter Tompkins's son, Edmund the Fourth, who was born in Oxford in 1826. When only twenty, he beat W. J. Cox in a match on the Merton Street court which lasted for more than four hours. Shortly afterwards, at the same age, he left to take up an appointment as the first professional at a newly built court in Leamington. Three years later he moved to London to take over the lease of the James Street court from W. J. and George Cox, to whom it had been passed down by their father.

The most important clashes between the champions and would-be champions of the day were staged in James Street, and the position of lessee, held for so long by Oxford men, was the most prestigious open to a professional. The court dated from 1635, when it was built in the fashionable Haymarket area of the West End by the Earl of Pembroke's barber, no doubt under his lordship's patronage. In the nineteenth century it lay in the heart of clubland.

Among Edmund the Fourth's hard-fought matches was a series of challenges on even terms against the French *paumier* known as Biboche, ranked second only to Barre. They played twice in Merton Street, twice in James Street and once in Biboche's Passage Sandrié court in Paris. Biboche's match-winning speciality was a high drop service spun so severely that it clung to the side wall, and this brought him a narrow victory on each occasion.

Julian Marshall, a contemporary historian of tennis who was well acquainted with Edmund the Fourth's game, made this analysis of it and paid this tribute to his artistry:

> Little need be said here of the style of this distinguished player, familiar as it is to the eyes of the whole Tennis-world. Though possessed of some effective and varied service, of a good *force* both boasted and direct, and a sure and well-cut volley, these are not his strongest points. The main strength of his game lies in his great judgment, clean cut, accurate length of stroke, great presence of mind, and indomitable perseverance; he may be said never to have known when he was beaten. His style, however, appears to modern critics to belong somewhat to an elder school of Tennis: pretty, graceful, and almost perfect as it is, so far as it goes, it is a complete contrast, and must yield in effectiveness, though not in beauty, to the more modern school of greater dash, force and severity.[7]

Such were the qualities which led the most successful of all the Tompkins family, at the age of thirty-six, to official recognition as the best player in the world. He was the last great representative of old-style tennis, before forcing overcame delicacy of stroke play and took the tennis world by storm. At the dawn of the era of the power game when taut stringing became a necessity, he preferred an old-fashioned racket loosely strung and would even tread on a new one to make it slacker. Stroking the ball to a length, rather than striking it, was his game.

He dethroned Edmond Barre in 1862 and came home to Oxford in triumph as World Champion four years later. The title was his until 1871, when a sprained ankle prevented him from accepting a challenge and he was forced to concede it to George

Lambert, another player who had learned the game in Merton Street.

In Oxford Edmund resumed the family's proprietorship of the Merton Street court by buying back from Thomas Sabin the lease which Sabin had bought from his father, Peter. His younger brother John was still running Peter's court in Brighton, and he was joined there by another brother, Alfred, who had been Edmund's assistant professional in James Street: in Brighton he built and managed a rackets court.

In later years Edmund progressively gave up competitive play but continued to coach and inspire undergraduates. In 1882 he handed over the management of the court to his assistant, William Webb, but remained involved and active even then: playing, however, 'more *en amateur* than *en artiste*'.[8]

In 1887 the lease was transferred to the name of J. H. Dickinson, who had married Edmund's eldest daughter, and in the following year Webb moved to the Manchester club. With the family succession assured, Edmund retired to Brighton to spend his last years with his brothers and their families. There he lived on until 1905, dying in his eightieth year.

Dickinson retained the lease until his death in 1923, when it passed to his son, R. C. E. (Reginald) Dickinson. This grandson of Edmund the Fourth was well qualified for his inheritance. He came to it after serving as head professional at Prince's Club in Knightsbridge, which, with two tennis and two rackets courts, had taken James Street's place as the pre-eminent tennis club in London.

The long reign of the Tompkins dynasty in Merton Street ended with the expiry of the younger Dickinson's lease in 1930, but by then the tradition of this philoprogenitive clan had extended to a wider world. Of John's seventeen children, two became tennis and

Chapter 10

rackets professionals: Alfred in Manchester and New York; Frederick at Prince's, with the Duke of Wellington at Stratfield Saye and then on to Malta and, finally, Philadelphia – far cries from Oxfordshire village life in Waterperry.[9]

CHAPTER 11

The Nineteenth-Century Renaissance

As demonstrated by the increasing mobility among professional players, tennis was once again growing in popularity. Throughout the course of the nineteenth century new courts were being built in England and, for almost the first time, outside Europe. This was in contrast to its dwindling in France, the cradle of the game. There the total number of courts in play during the century fluctuated from no more than nine to fewer than half a dozen.

In the previous century, when records began, all the World Champions had come from France. Philip Cox of Oxford was the first Englishman to hold the title. His triumph in 1819, followed by that of Edmund Tompkins (the Fourth) in 1862, heralded the Anglo-Saxon dominance of the game which has persisted to the present day. In the rest of continental Europe play continued for a time in courts at Geneva, Turin, Vienna and St Petersburg, but in countries where, as in France, tennis had once been all the rage – in Spain, in Germany and most of Italy – the game was all but extinct.

In England, where revolution had been averted and society had survived the threat of a Napoleonic invasion, the nobility continued to thrive and tennis once again became fashionable in its earliest manifestation as the preserve of the highest in the land. The lower classes were represented only by the professionals, whose status was generally that of servants.

Private courts were erected at ducal seats at Goodwood (Richmond and Gordon), Woburn (Bedford), Stratfield Saye (Wellington) and East Sheen (Fife), and by marquesses, earls and barons at Petworth House, Coombe Abbey, Hewell Grange, Hatfield House and Brougham Hall.

The wealthy and lesser titled emulated this example and other courts sprang up in gardens and grounds, beside stables or balancing orangeries on the wings of classical facades, at (amongst others) Easton Neston, Theobald's, Canford, Jesmond Dene, Moreton Morrell, Hayling Island and – in the vicinity of Oxford – Heythrop, Hardwick and Holyport.

When in London, players were catered for in private clubs. The most notable of these was the one in James Street, but this closed in 1866 against the trend. The building was then converted to ever humbler uses, ending ignominiously before demolition as a garage for Westminster City Council dust-carts. The former headquarters of the king of games is now commemorated only in the name of a neighbouring public house – The Hand and Racket in Orange Street (formerly James Street) – and by the benches which Edmund Tompkins brought with him when he returned to Oxford. These relics have accommodated spectators in the Merton Street dedans ever since in what has been accurately described as antique discomfort.

Compensation for the loss of James Street was forthcoming in the growth of other London clubs, all with fittingly aristocratic-sounding names: Lord's (in St John's Wood), Prince's (in Knightsbridge) and Queen's (in West Kensington). Outside London the formerly royal court at Hampton Court Palace was in use as a club, and new club courts at Brighton (1836), Leamington (1846) and Manchester (1880) supplemented those at Oxford and Cambridge.

By 1865 the revival had resulted in a total of twelve private and ten club courts in active use. By 1914 the number had risen to twenty-five in England as well as two in Scotland and one in

Ireland. Thus Oxonians graduating with an acquired taste for the game could readily find facilities for postgraduate play, and this, as in Elizabethan times, brought with it the social advantage of entry into the best society.

At the university, when doubts were raised about the suitability of some sporting activities, tennis won approval at the highest level. In a letter dated 17 February 1825 the Vice-Chancellor (Richard Jenkins) wrote to the Chancellor (Lord Grenville) deploring 'a more than becoming taste for pugilistic exercises' and fearing that 'any system of Gymnastics . . . may have the effect of indirectly promoting habits unfriendly to the great objects of our Academical institutions.' But 'I must also add,' he continued, 'that . . . ample opportunity is afforded by several courts for the manly amusement of tennis.'[1]

Of the 'several' (that is, three) courts in play in the 1820s, the once fair and stately building in Blue Boar Lane was nearing the end of its life and the court in Merton Street, after its rebuilding in 1798, was the most modern and acknowledged to be the best. This was vouched for in the memoirs of George Webbe Dasent and those of Charles Wordsworth, a Christ Church man, who also claimed the honour of teaching 'the same fine old English, or rather Anglo-Gallican, game' to Henry Denison, also of Christ Church, who 'had the credit, I believe, of being the best gentleman player in England'.[2]

When the Blue Boar court was no more, Oriel Street's came to be referred to as the old court and Merton Street's as the new. In his reminiscences of the 1830s Dasent, a cost-conscious undergraduate at Magdalen Hall, complained that 'Duck-legged Jem, the marker of the Old Court, sucked no small advantage out of us'. The Oriel Street professional is brought to life by an anecdote which Dasent relates:

> He was a character in his way. Nothing irritated him so much as when beginners whom he had taught went away to the new and much better court in Merton Lane. His was the old court, in Oriel Lane. I remember well when we began to desert his arena for the new court, he met us once coming out of the rival establishment, and I can still recall the look, more in sorrow than in anger, with which he said to Irwin –
>
> 'Oh, Mr Irwin, to think that I should see you coming out of this court! You, who have been used to play in my court, which have been trod by the feet of his sacred Majesty King Charles the First.'[3]

But Dasent believed that, since the Merton Street court had become the bigger and airier of the two, with a more even floor, his sacred Majesty would also have deserted poor Duck-legged Jem's for the superior venue.

Nevertheless it was to the Oriel Street court, for Jem's tuition, that the next king to play in Oxford went. During his year at the university the future Edward VII was formally an undergraduate at Christ Church, but in practice secluded in Frewen Hall at his father's insistence, to minimise the risk of his mixing in undesirable company.

On 28 October 1859 Colonel Bruce, the prince's Governor, made this report from Oxford to Queen Victoria:

> I do think that both morally and physically it is for his advantage that he should join in active games and amusement. There is a certain shrinking from exertion and exposure which I am anxious to combat. Therefore I am inclined to encourage rackets, tennis and suchlike . . .[4]

The Nineteenth-Century Renaissance

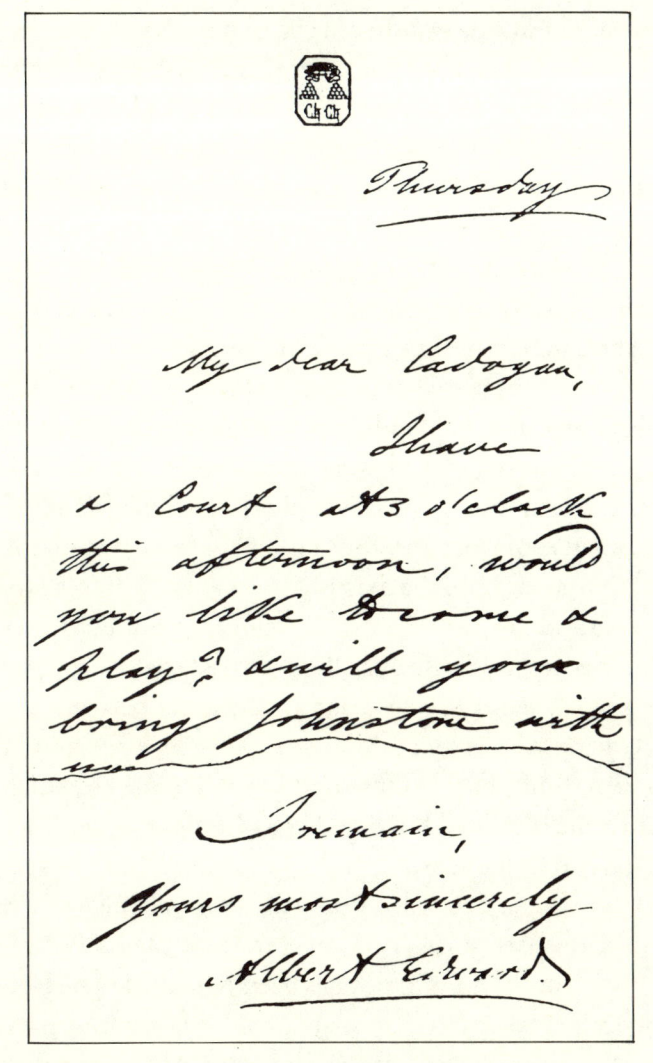

Thursday

My dear Cadogan,

I have a Court at 3 o'clock this afternoon, would you like to come & play? & will you bring Johnstone with you.

I remain,
Yours most sincerely
Albert Edward

Extract from a Letter from the Future King Edward VII

Accordingly, at one or other of the two tennis courts, the Prince of Wales played the game with members of his select circle, most often with the Earl of Cadogan and Sir Frederick Johnstone.

As a self-confessed 'poor hand' at the game, the prince liked it to be known when he won. In a letter to the earl dated 15 December 1859 he wrote: 'I was very sorry that our game at Tennis did not come off... I managed to get Mills to play & we had a capital two match [singles], we played six sets, & I was successful enough to win four against his two.'[5]

Twelve months later he and his suite patronised a crowded exhibition benefit match held in the Merton Street court for the unfortunate James Russell when his less favoured establishment in Oriel Street was degenerating into no more than a billiards salon.

The expense of the game was still a cause of complaint in the 1850s. Charges at both the existing courts were felt to be too steep for undergraduates, and the future Dean Fremantle, Master of the Temple, was among those at Balliol who assisted in organising the building of rackets and fives courts on ground between the Parks and St Giles as a cheaper alternative.[6] Subsequently, more rackets courts were built, but too few undergraduates were attracted to the game. The Holywell Racquet Court Company was bankrupted before the end of the century, and no court in the city has survived.

Competitive play between Oxford and Cambridge at what was by far the longest-established game in both places began at this time, much later than might have been expected. The honour of precedence in Varsity matches had been usurped in the 1820s by two relative newcomers, cricket and rowing. The trend towards team games in the public schools and universities was then developing, and it may also be that tennis was slow to be recognised as an official university game because neither university possessed facilities of its own. In the mid-nineteenth century the two surviving Oxford courts, soon to be one, were still what they had always been: privately owned commercial ventures, open to all comers possessing the wherewithal to pay the court fees.

In 1850 an annual singles competition for an Oxford Prize Racquet, open only to undergraduates, was inaugurated at Merton Street by the keeper, Thomas Sabin. It was a Gold Racquet until 1856 and a Silver Racquet thereafter. Annual matches between the two universities followed in 1859, with the Prize Racquet holder qualifying as Oxford's first string.

The relative strength of tennis-playing in the colleges may be assessed from the names of these Prize Racquet holders. By this yardstick Christ Church is shown to be the dominant college with nineteen winners between 1850 and 1914, followed by Balliol with twelve and New College with ten. The rest of the field was far behind, headed by Oriel and University College with four each and Magdalen and Merton with three. All these, it may be noted, were among the more fashionable of the colleges at this period.

When inaugurated, the Varsity matches consisted of one singles and one four-handed (doubles) match, each to the best of five sets. The first string, a full blue, played in both; the second string, a half blue, only in the doubles until 1912 when a second singles was played for the first time, although not officially part of the fixture until 1922.

The earliest matches were played in London in the James Street court. After its closure the fixture was transferred to Lord's. There it was usually scheduled to coincide with the Varsity or Eton and Harrow cricket match, and this brought the benefit of attracting large numbers of spectators. Dedans, side galleries and top gallery were all crowded to capacity. The professionals on each side were permitted to attend, but restrained from imparting advice during the course of play.

Like Oxford, Cambridge had seen tennis fall out of fashion in the eighteenth century and the college courts pulled down, but a comparison of the facilities available to undergraduates in the nineteenth century was greatly in Cambridge's favour. There the renaissance, which was so little in evidence in Oxford, bore fruit. The Pembroke College court survived until 1880 and, while at Oxford the court in Oriel Street was struggling against closure, at Cambridge a new public court beside Parker's Piece, the Wellington, opened in 1854. Afterwards, when play in Oxford was restricted to a single, no longer modern, court, Cambridge undergraduates were treated to a brand-new pair. The first Clare and Trinity court in Grange Road was built in 1866 and the second in 1890.

This superiority in number and quality of courts was reflected in the results of matches played in the annual encounters. The fixture ran without a break between 1859 and 1914 except for a gap in 1864, and during that period Oxford won the singles eighteen times to Cambridge's thirty-seven and the doubles twenty times to Cambridge's thirty-five: an average of almost two to one in Cambridge's favour. Curiously, whenever one side failed to win both singles and doubles there was no deciding play-off: the match was declared drawn.

Christ Church was the Oxford college most represented during this period, followed by New College, Balliol, Magdalen and University College. Among schools there was a heavy preponderance of Etonians on both sides. The most distinguished Oxford player was Sir Edward Grey (Winchester and Balliol), later six times Amateur Champion and later still Foreign Secretary and Earl Grey of Fallodon. Two others went on to win the Amateur Championship, but overall Cambridge attracted the most outstanding talent, nurturing champions of the calibre of the Hon.

Alfred Lyttelton, Eustace Miles and Edgar Baerlein. Oxford's greater strength lay in the superiority of its professionals.

Thomas Sabin's interregnum as keeper of the Merton Street court, interrupting the long reign of the Tompkins dynasty, lasted for thirty years. During those years other buildings were developed on the site and the property grew correspondingly more valuable, increasingly expensive to maintain under a full repairing lease, and more tempting to capitalise. As well as the court itself, the lease which was drawn up in August 1847 covered a 'newly erected tenement' with a kitchen, stable and coach house and a 'lately erected building' used as dressing rooms.[7]

This lease, which was non-assignable, was in the name of Sabin's father, William, who had evidently borne the cost of at least the new dressing rooms. When he died the following year, it was bequeathed to his executor, John Fisher, who was a builder (as perhaps William Sabin had been). But in 1859 Merton College, still the freeholder, granted a licence which allowed it to be assigned to a third party: a tailor named John Embling.

Embling's interest did not last long. Only three years later, in January 1862, Fisher, who appears to have been acting as a trustee, surrendered the lease of the property (which now included two fives courts) 'to the intent a new lease might be granted to Thomas Wm. Sabin'.[8] In February a new lease, for forty years at £20 a year, was duly granted to him. On this occasion it was assignable, and only six months later Sabin assigned it to Frederick Morrell, gentleman.[9]

Frederick Morrell was a solicitor, a member of the wealthy Oxford family of brewers and lawyers. Presumably he had sufficient capital to pay Sabin a lump sum for the assignment. This may have been simply an investment, but it seems more likely that Morrell was acting as an angel because Sabin needed ready money, could not afford to hold on to the lease himself, and wanted it in friendly hands. Certainly, when Sabin retired in December 1866, Morrell behaved most obligingly in assigning it to Edmund Tompkins the Fourth, then living near Hampton Court ('of East Moulsey, gentleman').[10]

Seven years later, in April 1873, Tompkins, like Sabin, evidently found possession of the whole property too burdensome. He obtained a licence to assign the lease to Charles Wadlow, a veterinary surgeon, while retaining use of the court. Tompkins was again described as a gentleman, now residing, probably in some comfort on his earnings from court fees and exhibition matches, in the Oxfordshire village of Upper Heyford.[11]

Keepers could seldom manage their courts singlehanded, and among the various assistant professionals, markers and apprentices employed at Merton Street by Sabin and Edmund the Fourth were three rising stars destined for fame in the annals of tennis: George Lambert, Thomas Stone and Edward Hunt.

Lambert came from a family which challenged even the Tompkinses in size and talent. Down the generations each supplied the game with ten professionals, and it was George who took the crown of World Champion from Edmund the Fourth. The respect in which both families were held was demonstrated when the Laws of Tennis were formulated in 1877 to standardise rules of play throughout the growing number of clubs and courts. These were submitted to four leading professionals for comment and endorsement before being finalised for adoption. George and Edmund were two of the élite consulted; the others were Edmund's brothers, John and Alfred.

The first of the Lamberts had been in the service of the Marquess of Salisbury in the post of Groom to the Chambers at Hatfield House, where there was (and is) a tennis court. George, his grandson, succeeded his brother Thomas in an apprenticeship in Merton Street. Between 1859 and 1866 he learned and practised his skills under the expert tutelage of Edward Hunt, a superlative coach who was at the Oxford court from the mid-1850s until 1874, first as Sabin's assistant and then as Edmund the Fourth's.

On completion of his seven-year apprenticeship in Oxford, George Lambert moved to Hampton Court and then on to Lord's, which was James Street's first successor as the headquarters of the game. There he was appointed head professional at a wage of £2 a week. Stocky and muscular, he became known from his forceful style of play, so different from that of Edmund Tompkins, as the forerunner of the modern school of play. With an arm and wrist of steel, he perfected the art of propelling a severely cut ball at great speed. It was in 1871, at the age of twenty-nine, that he challenged Edmund for the World Championship. Out of practice after spraining an ankle, Edmund conceded the title without a match, and so great was George's acknowledged pre-eminence that he held it for the next fourteen years unchallenged.

The contribution to the game made by Thomas Stone, who had accompanied Edmund Tompkins from James Street to Oxford in 1868, was less brilliant than George Lambert's but more far-reaching. The English-speaking take-over of the game was now to be consolidated by its export from England to Australia and the United States, and in each case Oxford was called upon to provide the knowledge and skills demanded in those virgin territories.

The honour of introducing tennis to Australia belongs to Samuel Smith Travers, who built the first court in the southern hemisphere, and to Stone, whom he enticed from Oxford to be its keeper, play with him and teach his friends. It was at first a private court, but soon became a club under Stone's management.

According to the account of Smith Travers in Noel and Clark's

A History of Tennis, 'this gentleman, whose home was in Hobart Town, Tasmania, learned the game and became deeply enamoured of it in his Oxford University days'.[12] But in fact he was an Englishman, not an Australian, and was never a member of the university at Oxford, as the records of those matriculating testify. A partner in a long-established family firm in the City of London, he played his tennis mostly in James Street, and it is there that Stone may first have come to his notice.

The connection with Oxford was literary. Smith Travers engaged in a voluminous correspondence with Henry Sides, an assistant librarian at the Bodleian, whom he employed as research assistant for his *Collection of Pedigrees of the Family of Travers* (1864). This was published by Parker's (then 'of the Cornmarket'), and Smith Travers's Foreword was dated from Oxford. (His more relevant work, *A Treatise on Tennis*, was published from Hobart Town in 1875.)

Thomas Stone was born in 1839, the son of a lamp-lighter at Hampton Court Palace, where he began his tennis career as a boy and an assistant professional. At the age of twenty he moved to London to become Edmund Tompkins's assistant in James Street. Whilst there, he marked the epic five-day World Championship match between Tompkins and Edmond ('Papa') Barre which ended in a draw and Barre conceding the title. When the court closed in 1866, Stone followed Tompkins to Oxford.

Smith Travers emigrated to Tasmania in 1870; the building of his court was not finished until 1874; and Stone arrived from Oxford early the following year. The cost of bringing him out and employing him was evidently contentious. In November 1874 Smith Travers wrote to the manager of the Travers sugar estate in Queensland:

> Thank you much for writing Thos. Stone, the tennis marker. 'Mum' is the word about this. He will be paid for by the Club I am forming. Still, my dear brother would be irritated to hear of it. I do it not for the mere love of tennis, but for exercise and to prolong my valuable life by the bi-weekly sweat. As one gets old it is impossible to take exercise unless supported by the stimulus of excitement.[13]

The court was modelled on the one in James Street, and the situation suited Stone. He decided to settle, and his wife came out to join him eighteen months later, despite finding it 'hard to say goodbye to all at home'.[14]

Smith Travers's choice of professional turned out so well and his enthusiasm was so infectious that a court was built in Melbourne and Stone was employed to manage it – at a higher salary of £250 a year plus 10% of the court fees. The parting from Hobart was said to be without ill-feeling. Stone remained at Melbourne as manager and secretary of the club from 1882 until his death forty-two years later at the age of eighty-five. His second tennis career had lasted even longer than his first; together they spanned more than seventy years.

For more than a century since Smith Travers's initiative, the Oxford connection with tennis in Australia has been maintained by returning Rhodes Scholars and other Australian graduates who have been introduced to the game during their time at the university. They have contributed a regular infusion of new blood into their home clubs in Hobart, Melbourne and, latterly, Ballarat. Today, despite the small number of courts (four in all), Australian dedication to sport has triumphed in tennis and Australian professionals have made themselves the best players in the world. In a reciprocal gesture to Oxford, Australia has even provided a professional to teach the game to undergraduates in Merton Street.

Just as Samuel Smith Travers transported Thomas Stone and tennis to Australia, so in the following year a Bostonian, Hollis Horatio Hunnewell, shipped out another professional from Oxford, this time Edward Hunt, to bring the game to another continent.

Hunnewell was a trail-blazer. In Boston he built the first modern court in America, and he is also credited with being the first person in the United States to wear a bowler hat.[15] The court which he built, with Nathaniel Thayer, in 1876 was a private one in Buckingham Street. What he initiated thereby was the successful revival of a game which had been played in New York in colonial times. There are recorded references to games of tennis (being forbidden during divine service) in an edict by the Governor in 1659; to the sale of a court by auction in 1763; and to the importing of 'best racquets for tennis and fives' in 1766.[16]

Like Thomas Stone, Ted Hunt was not himself a great player but an excellent coach, and he has a double claim to remembrance by posterity. In addition to his role as America's pioneer professional, he is the only man who has taught the game to two World Champions on different continents: George Lambert in Oxford and Tom Pettitt in Boston.

Pettitt was an English immigrant boy employed to assist Hunt in the Boston court. As he grew, he was reputed to be as strong as a lion and quick as a panther, and his talent developed prodigiously under Hunt's tuition. Indeed he advanced the power game so far ahead of his time that his hitting of the ball was condemned by exponents of the classic game as wild and barbaric. He was once even accused of almost murdering an opponent with the ferocity of his returns.

The Nineteenth-Century Renaissance

In 1885 Pettitt came to England to challenge George Lambert for the world title. The match took place at Hampton Court over a period of three days. Lambert was in the lead after two, but he was aged forty-five and tiring. Pettitt recovered from three sets to five down to beat him on the third day by seven sets to five (a total of 361 winning strokes to 352). In less than a decade Hunt and his young prodigy had put America in the forefront of the game.

Ted Hunt was the first of many of his kind to travel west. Rich Anglophiles in the United States had caught the fever for tennis from the upper class in England, and a steady flow of members of the established families of English professionals – Tompkinses, Whites, Forresters, Johnsons – crossed the Atlantic in his wake to manage newly built courts and provide the best rackets, balls and instruction in return for higher wages and better conditions than they could expect at home. Hunt's own eventual fate was a sad one. Although in old age he made the journey home to Oxford to die, he never saw the city or court again because he was blind.

In all, eighteen courts were built in the United States between 1876 and 1923, when the last of them opened in Chicago. Of these no fewer than fifteen were sited in the eastern states in the area of Boston, New York and Philadelphia. Most were club courts, but the millionaire Gould family built themselves a private one, described as palatial, and the Whitneys, not to be outclassed, two.

Today nine remain. In the New York Racquet and Tennis Club at 370 Park Avenue there are two courts on the top storey of a splendid Venetianesque palazzo dating from 1918. Boston and Philadelphia have one each, also centrally situated and also affording luxurious facilities of a kind never seen in Oxford. There is a court at the former summer resort of New York society, Newport,

Rhode Island, and another at the exclusive Tuxedo Country Club in New York state (where the dinner jacket was first worn in America; hence its American name). The Whitney court at Manhasset, Long Island, and the former Gould court at Lakewood, New Jersey, are in only occasional use, but the former Whitney court at Aiken, South Carolina, remains in active use as a club.

Tennis in the United States has been handicapped not only by its failure to spread to the west but also by the lack of a court at any of the Ivy League universities. An introduction to the game is therefore not available to potential players at the most appropriate of venues and at the ideal age for learning how best to wield a racket. Thus the game is deprived of a regular influx of new recruits such as those supplied by Oxford and Cambridge, long known as 'the chief strongholds of the game in England'.[17]

The expense and esoteric nature of tennis, too, have contributed to the paucity of courts and players in America, but among the small number of enthusiasts the general standard of play has risen to remarkable heights. This has been achieved through recruitment of the most expert of professional coaching wherever it was to be found. The first wave of Hunt's successors were English. Their replacements were, increasingly, home-bred. Some, more recently, have been French and Australian.

Pierre Etchebaster, the last French holder of the world title (from 1928 to 1952), was appointed head tennis professional at the New York club on his retirement from competitive play, and that post is currently held (1994) by the reigning World Champion, Wayne Davies of Australia.

The roll of American World Champions, inspired by the example of Tom Pettitt, is impressive. With the advantage of his own court and his own professional, and blessed with a natural talent

*James Russell ('Duck-Legged Jem'),
Keeper of the Oriel Street Court*

Edmund Tompkins the Fourth, World Champion 1862–71

*World Champions, Tom Pettitt (1885–90)
and George Lambert (right) (1871–85)*

Thomas Stone, the Pioneer of Tennis in Australia

*Father and Son: Lord Aberdare and Hon. M.G.L. Bruce
(the Present Lord Aberdare), Oxford Blues and Amateur Champions*

Chris Ronaldson, World Champion 1981–87
[Photo Mike Roberts]

*Richard Montgomerie, Captain of Tennis 1994,
at the Hazard End of the Merton Street Court*
[Photo Robin Mayes, Times Newspapers Ltd]

Oxford University Women's Team 1994
Back row: Lucinda Cannon Brookes (Worcester)
Kees Ludekens (Coach), Anne-Marie Moody (Oriel)
Front row: Jo Dixon (Wadham), Ailsa Hart (Capt., Merton)
Kate Owers (Green)

which was the wonder of the tennis world, Jay Gould became, in 1914, the first amateur ever to win the title. Three other American amateurs – Northrup Knox and the Bostwick brothers, Pete and Jimmy – followed in an unbroken succession between 1959 and 1976.

Such were the fruits of the nineteenth-century revival of this ancient game brought via Oxford to two new continents.

CHAPTER 12

Modern Times in Oxford

THE FIRST World War brought the Varsity matches to a halt. Throughout the country at large it marked the close of an affluent era of court-building and expansion which was on the wane. Already at the turn of the century Eustace Miles, the Amateur Champion, in emphasising the social value of tennis because 'not a little of it is connected with the life in English country-houses', had lamented that tennis house-parties were not so frequent as they had been.[1]

Neither the social cachet of the game nor the upper-class life to which it had become attached were to be fully restored. At some country-house courts – Hatfield, Petworth, Holyport, Moreton Morrell, for example – clubs were formed, open to any player willing and able to pay the annual subscription and court fees. Restricted by the number of courts and the prohibitive cost of building new ones for so few players, tennis was still very much a minority sport but no longer so socially exclusive.

Indeed during the course of the twentieth century the game progressively regained a small measure of the popularity which it had enjoyed in the sixteenth. In the 1950s three ducal courts, long unused – at Stratfield Saye, Woburn and Goodwood – finally disappeared, but in the latter half of the century the number of players overall multiplied and wherever courts were available they were used far more intensively than ever before.

The Varsity matches were revived in 1920. Two years later the second-string matches achieved official recognition, so that, with two singles and one doubles, there was an end to draws. For the next ten years, between 1922 and 1931, Cambridge maintained a crushing superiority, winning all twenty singles matches and eight out of the ten doubles. But this was followed by a succession of Oxford victories from 1932 to 1938.

When the fixture was resumed in 1947 after the Second World War the results were at first more even; then Cambridge became dominant in the 1960s and Oxford in the 1970s. From 1976 the number of matches in the fixture was increased to four singles and two doubles. Instead of one full and one half blue, four half blues were awarded.

Oxford blues between and after the two wars included D. R. Jardine, later a controversial England cricket captain, and four players talented enough to represent the university at first string for three years: V. A. Cazalet, C. S. Crawley, P. V. F. Cazalet and R. C. Riseley. The only player to better their achievement was A. C. Lovell, who represented the university for four years from 1973 to 1976 at first string.

Robert Riseley went on to become the MCC Gold Racquet holder in 1950 and Amateur Champion in 1955. Alan Lovell won the MCC Gold Racquet eight times and the amateur championship five times during the 1980s. He also served for thirteen years in the senior administrative role of Chairman of The Tennis and Rackets Association's Tennis Committee.

Outstanding among other distinguished Oxford blues have been a father and son: the Hon. C. N. Bruce, later the third Lord Aberdare, and the Hon. M. G. L. Bruce, who succeeded him in the title. The father was Oxford's first string in 1906 and 1908, won the MCC Gold Racquet five times in the 1930s and became Amateur Champion in 1932 and 1938. The son was Oxford's first string in 1939 after winning the Oxford Silver Racquet in 1938. (It is now on loan to the Wimbledon Lawn Tennis Museum.) He won the MCC Gold Racquet five times in succession from 1954 to 1958 and the Amateur Championship four times during the same years. Since then he has given invaluable service to the two games as President of The Tennis and Rackets Association (and to the House of Lords as Chairman of Committees).

In January 1900, when Merton College leased the tennis and fives courts and a 'dwelling house' in Merton Street to Edmund Tompkins the Fourth's son-in-law, John Dickinson, the rent was £85 per annum and the lease was to run only from year to year. Dickinson had kept the court since 1887 and continued to do so for a further ten years, assisted by Edward Gray. But in 1910 he handed over the keepership to Duncan Wilson and after him, in 1912, to William Cass, while retaining the lease of all the property himself. In 1919, when a new lease was granted to his son, Reginald, the dwelling house was not included and the annual rent was reduced to £70.

Fifteen years later an end was at last put to this, by then long-outdated, arrangement whereby the only court available to members of the university was owned and managed by an individual lessee as a family business. On 11 July 1934 a lease was granted to the Hon. Ian Leslie Melville and the Rev. Maurice Roy Ridley as trustees for the Oxford University Tennis Club. The annual rent remained unchanged at £70, but the lease was terminable at three months' notice by either party. Bill Cass, although still the keeper, then became an employee of the club. A good coach but an unsatisfactory manager, he became noted for his lugubriousness and known to undergraduates in the late 1930s as 'Miserable Cass'.

After the two royal courts, at Falkland Palace (1539) and Hampton Court (rebuilt on its present site in the 1620s), Oxford's was then the oldest in use and showing its age. A new floor had been laid and some renovation undertaken in 1912, but otherwise the lease-holding professionals appear to have been unable or unwilling to bear the cost of more than a bare minimum of maintenance ever since the rebuilding in 1798. For some years before 1934 no money at all had been spent on the amenities, such as they were. Maurice Ridley, a Fellow of Balliol, roundly declared them to be non-existent.

Once the lease was in its possession, the club set about putting the changing room to rights with a new floor and a shower. The light through the court windows was so dim that play was impossible after three o'clock on winter afternoons, and this was remedied by the installation of electric lighting in the flat ceiling beneath the roof beams.[2]

The stimulus engendered by these improvements was abruptly halted by the outbreak of war five years later. Bill Cass departed and was not replaced. The war years were succeeded by post-war austerity and a shortage of both funds and trained professionals. Without a resident professional for more than twenty years, tennis at Oxford sank to its lowest ebb for centuries. With little instruction or encouragement to entice them, few of the gifted games-playing undergraduates of that period tried their hand at the intellectually most challenging of ball games.

Merton granted the club a new lease in 1946, still at £70 per annum, but this time for an initial twelve months with a notice period of six months thereafter. It was signed on behalf of OUTC by Arthur Goodhart, Fellow (later Master) of University College, and Maurice Baring. In 1955 the fives courts were demolished and the land on which they stood was removed from the tenancy to become part of the garden of Grove House in Kybald Lane. Entrance to the court was then changed from Grove House Yard in Kybald Lane to Stable Yard in Merton Street. In 1974 it was changed again, to the present entrance through the car park behind Old Warden's Lodgings.

In the late 1940s and the 1950s the game was kept alive in Oxford through the dedication of a small number of resident enthusiasts, notably Arthur Goodhart, who acted as the club's Senior Treasurer, Michael Maclagan, the senior tutor of Trinity, and Micky Jones, the bursar of the Dragon School (who was also *The Times* Tennis Correspondent). Leading players of the day came to the rescue with visits to the court to arouse interest by demonstrating the excitement of the game. In 1946/47, for example, the galleries were crowded to watch an exhibition match between two former Amateur Champions, Lord Aberdare and W. D. Macpherson, and another between the reigning Amateur Champion, Lowther Lees, and a senior professional, Henry Johns.

During the post-war years, too, some essential part-time coaching was provided by R. J. Lay, the rackets professional at Radley, and after him by Jack Groom, the head professional at Lord's, who paid weekly visits.

In 1961 Peter Ellis, a young professional at Queen's Club in West Kensington, was recruited, but for the winter months only. Finding the journey from London tedious and parts of the club premises almost derelict, he left after two seasons, and there was no replacement. Yet, with undergraduate captains and secretaries changing year by year, OUTC, even more than other clubs, felt the need for a permanent, full-time professional.

In these circumstances concern for the future of tennis in Oxford led to decisive action by four former Oxford players who met regularly while playing at Lord's. Reginald Graham, Lord Aberdare, Mark Baring and the Earl of Kinnoull persuaded Peter Dawes, an assistant at the Lord's court, to take on the neglected court in Merton Street. It was Graham who, in the first of many generous benefactions to the Oxford club, made the move possible by lending this young professional the money to buy a house in Oxford.

The arrival in 1965 of the first full-time professional since 1939 brought the post-war era to a long overdue close. Dawes took charge of a dismally run-down building, and his energies were at first devoted largely to painting and decorating. The fabric of the court was in disrepair, broken windows needed mending, and there was no heating: a gas fire installed several years earlier had never been connected to the mains. In the evenings the court was used for badminton. The number of active tennis players was ten.

But Dawes (later to become first Chairman of the Real Tennis Professionals Association) proved an inspired choice. When he was able to turn from being a general handyman to recruiting new players among the undergraduates, he made an introductory offer of three free lessons, and in a remarkably short time the court was so fully booked during term-time that hour-long sessions had to be reduced to forty-five minutes.

An off-court hazard on the premises in Merton Street is a dark flight of steep and awkwardly twisting stairs leading up to the club and changing rooms. Peter Dawes was by no means the first or last person to fall at this hazard, but in doing so he suffered the misfortune of a hip injury which kept him off the court for a long period and left him with a permanent limp. Yet even with this handicap he remained agile and robust enough to win an exhibition match against the Amateur Champion, Howard Angus, after saving five match points.

As the number of players increased, membership fell more distinctly into three categories: undergraduate, don and local resident. OUTC, the leaseholder of the court, was a university club subject to the jurisdiction of the proctors, but membership could not be restricted because there was no prospect of financial viability without the contributions of senior members and non-university players to subsidise undergraduate play.

The first of three attempts to regularise the constitutional position was made in 1967 through the formation of a separate club. This was founded and presided over until 1978 by the bursar of University College, Vice-Admiral Sir Peter Gretton. In that capacity and later as OUTC's Senior Treasurer, Admiral Gretton, a hero of the Second World War, became the leading stalwart of post-war tennis in Oxford. To his wholehearted involvement and firm management is due a large share of the credit for its restoration to good health.

A picture of a unicorn is painted on the grille of the Merton Street court in remembrance of the inn where tennis had been played in Blue Boar Lane, and Oxford Unicorns was the name adopted by the university's second team. Somewhat confusingly, this mythical beast was chosen by the OUTC committee as the name of the new club for senior players. The Unicorn Club, otherwise the Oxford Unicorns Club, was to be a supporters' club with, as the committee minutes jocularly recorded, 'no connection with Oxford Unicorns!'[3] For the sake of clarity the term 'Oxford Seniors' was used instead to designate teams of members not in *stat. pup*.

With the court thriving, an assistant was required for Peter Dawes, and in 1971 the employment of one under The Tennis and Rackets Association's training scheme, financed by its Young Professionals Fund, was agreed. An advertisement in a local job centre produced a scruffy, long-haired, unshaven twenty-one-year-old who came straight from work on a building site to offer his services. Granted an interview despite appearances, he revealed himself to be a former pupil of Magdalen College School, an Oxfordshire junior lawn tennis champion and a prospective student at the University of Hawaii, which had offered him a lawn tennis scholarship. His name was Chris Ronaldson.

During his seven-year stint in Merton Street Dawes was brilliantly successful in inspiring a renewal of enthusiasm for tennis in Oxford, and he made another important contribution to the game when he decided to employ the young Ronaldson on a three months' trial. His appointment of this probationary assistant professional launched a fourth Oxford-bred World Champion on one of the most remarkable of tennis careers.

Dawes taught his recruit the basic technique of stroke play and the tactics of the game and was amazed at the speed with which they were absorbed and mastered. He also discovered that he had got himself a keen organiser in the management of the court. The prescribed training period was three years, abbreviated from the traditional seven-year apprenticeship. But when Dawes left to take up an appointment at the Seacourt club on Hayling Island, Ronaldson succeeded to the post of senior professional after only eight months.

By this time the number of playing members had risen to a hundred, but the club's finances were not in good shape. Small but worrying annual losses were being incurred. The professional's remuneration was static at £16 a week, supplemented by modest fees from coaching. To make a living, he was dependent on what income he could derive from operating the professional's room as a sports shop and taking on outside work, stringing squash and lawn tennis rackets.

Ronaldson had intended to become a lawn tennis coach, but took to the real game with such extraordinary zest and flair that he put all thought of lawn tennis and the University of Hawaii behind him. As a superlative sportsman and an inspiration to other players, he was a gift to the game and has amply repaid it for the pleasure and fame it has brought him.

His career was to be international, and his time in Oxford short. Towards the end of 1973 he accepted a post in Australia with the Royal Melbourne Tennis Club, which had sold its site in the city centre and was building new premises with two modern courts in the suburb of Richmond.

Like Oxford before the arrival of Peter Dawes, Melbourne was sorely in need of the services of an enthusiast with coaching and managerial skills. The club had been without a professional since the death of Thomas Stone's son, Woolner, ten years before. Now, stimulated by Ronaldson's drive and dedication in teaching and promoting the game, there was a rapid expansion in membership and a lasting revival of the game in Australia.

After five years he returned to Britain to help the game in Scotland by resuscitating the ailing Sun Court Hotel club in Troon. From there he moved to tennis's premier club, the Royal Tennis Court at Hampton Court, where he soon trebled the court bookings. Three years later he was seconded to Bordeaux at the head of an operation to rescue the club which, as in Melbourne, had moved from the city centre to a suburb. It had run into financial difficulties and was about to close, but he succeeded in reversing the decline and securing its future. In 1985 he was a leading Founder-Director of the revived Holyport club.

As a player Ronaldson took the title of World Champion from Howard Angus, the Cambridge amateur, in 1981 and held it until 1987. In 1984 he achieved a unique tally of Grand Slam victories, holding all four of tennis's Open Championships at the same time: the British, French, US and Australian. His skills as a coach found expression in *Tennis: A Cut above the Rest*, a manual of guidance for players published from Oxford in 1985.

In 1973 OUTC once again sought to redefine its position as a university club dependent on the support of non-university players. A new constitution was adopted proclaiming as its objective: 'to further the sport of Real Tennis in the University and City of Oxford'. This ruled that membership 'shall be open to all matriculated members of the University of Oxford, and in addition, such other members, known corporately as The Senior Unicorns Club, as the committee shall think fit'. As officers 'the club shall have a President, a Senior Treasurer, a Captain, a Secretary, a Captain of the University Second Team, and a Senior Unicorn Fixture Secretary', the Senior Treasurer to be a resident member of Congregation. The committee was to consist of these officers and three other members to be elected each year at the AGM.

Initially there was no President, Michael Maclagan retaining the designation of Chairman, while Admiral Gretton continued as Treasurer. Maclagan was honoured with the presidency in 1983, when he retired from the chairmanship. His successor in the chair was the Professor of Engineering, Peter Wroth, of Brasenose, who was to die tragically early five years later, following his move to Cambridge as Master of Emmanuel.

In February 1974 an Appeal was launched to return the court and premises to a state of lasting good repair and improve the facilities for members and the professional. Although Dawes and Ronaldson had raised numbers almost to maximum capacity, the need to keep subscriptions and court fees low had made it impossible to accumulate sufficient funds to carry out even essential maintenance work. Response to the Appeal enabled the necessary work to be completed in the course of the next three years.

In the tennis world generally, the division between amateur and professional had by this date ceased to be related to class and education. The best professionals were not only endowed with the high degree of intelligence necessary for success at tennis; their minds, unlike those of their predecessors, were trained by higher education. After school Ronaldson had attended the University of Kent. Mick Dean, his successor in Merton Street, was a graduate of Manchester University, who in 1977 resigned his appointment as professional to become a graduate student at Keble, reading for a Diploma of Education. He then pursued a teaching career as a master at Radley.

Like Ronaldson, Dean came to the game from lawn tennis. He became Ronaldson's assistant at the beginning of 1973 and, after a short spell at Lord's, returned to take over from him towards the end of the year. Under his management court bookings during term-time reached a hundred hours a week, and he helped to produce outstanding players in Alan Lovell and Peter Seabrook (the former Winchester rackets pair) and John Leslie, from Rugby, who was also to become World Squash Champion.

Dean's return to student life led to an event without parallel: a former professional playing in the Varsity match. By 1978 the match consisted of two doubles and four singles and, with Dean playing, Oxford won all six rubbers without losing a set. 'Arguments that he was ineligible were not strongly pursued,' commented *The Times* in reporting that this was the 107th match between the two universities 'and it is highly doubtful whether any of its predecessors have been so one-sided'.[4]

Oxford's new professional was Michael Flanagan, another good lawn tennis player, who came from the RAF. He was soon succeeded by Chris Ronaldson's brother Steve, and he in turn by Jerome Fletcher, assisted by Alan Oliver. Fletcher and Oliver were both Oxford graduates (Trinity and St Peter's respectively), although neither had been introduced to the game when undergraduates.

Oliver, who has served the club part-time since 1982, was a friend of Chris Ronaldson and had been, like him, a pupil at Magdalen College School and a county lawn tennis player for Oxfordshire. When Fletcher left, he was joined by Mark Eadle, a young Oxford United footballer who quickly took to tennis and after four years in Merton Street moved on in 1989 to the nearby court newly opened at the Oratory School. His replacement was Kees Ludekens, an Australian physical education instructor and tennis coach, recruited from Ballarat.

As indicated by this coming and going of professionals, generally self-employed, the club's finances were perpetually at too low an ebb to offer the promise or prospect of an attractive remuneration. Nor, crucially in a city where living costs were high, did the club own any residential accommodation. The problem was aggravated by part-time working and some necessary overlapping, which meant that two professionals were often being employed when the club could barely afford one. On the other hand, full staffing brought a greater utilisation of the court, particularly during vacations.

The root of the problem lay in the lack of provision of any facilities by the university. At Cambridge, by contrast, the university had acquired the remaining active Trinity and Clare court with adjacent house, where Brian Church, the head professional, has lived and provided expert and experienced tuition to successive generations of undergraduates for more than thirty years. At Oxford lawn tennis, squash and Eton and Rugby fives courts are available on the university's Iffley Road sports ground, but no courts have been built for the senior games of tennis and rackets – minority sports incurring a higher capital expenditure.

The survival of tennis in Oxford has therefore depended on the good will of the governing body of a single college, which would no doubt prefer to put such a conveniently situated building to residential or academic use, as has happened at Oriel. Since OUTC took on the lease it has enjoyed no security of tenure beyond a single year, although in recent years the court has become protected by listed-building status.

Understandably during times of inflation, Merton has required an ever-mounting annual rent. Although the college generously kept this below the level of city centre rents prevailing in the 1980s, it rose from £425 in 1979 to £500 in 1980, £750 in 1983, £1500 in 1986, £2000 in 1987 and £2500 in 1988. Even with donations and higher subscriptions and court fees from senior members, these steeply rising costs created a situation such as no other club in the university had been called upon to face.

Responsibility for managing the club's affairs and meeting this challenge rested with John Cook, a local businessman who had taken over management of the Oxford Seniors in 1968. He went on to serve as Senior Treasurer for eleven years, and the club was fortunate to have the benefit of his financial skills during the years of high inflation. He was elected Chairman in 1988 and subsequently President until succeeded in 1993 by Dr Gordon Baker, a philosopher at St John's.

Cook's successor as Senior Treasurer in 1988 was Dr Bruce Henning of St Catherine's, and supervision of the club's affairs has been in his very capable hands since then. Under his leadership the early 1990s proved eventful.

Thanks mainly to some excellent coaching by Kees Ludekens, the professional he had engaged from across the world, a series of Cambridge victories in Varsity matches during the 1980s was brought to an end. Oxford's victory in 1990 was a narrow one, but those in 1991 and 1992 were repetitions of the 1978 whitewash: in the total of twelve matches played, Cambridge did not win a single set. Oxford had found a new star in Roman Krznaric (Pembroke), and he was immediately followed by another, Richard Montgomerie (Worcester), who was also Captain of Cricket in 1994 and a county cricket player for Northamptonshire.

There was, too, another development in which Oxford could take pride. Down the centuries until the present age of sexual equality tennis remained an almost exclusively male preserve. Women players were rare phenomena. There was Margot from Hainault who created a sensation in Paris in 1427: 'She played both fore-handed and back-handed very powerfully, very cunningly, and very cleverly, as any man could, and there were but few men whom she could not beat.'[5] There was Mademoiselle Bunel, a regular opponent of the Prince de Condé around 1760, who attracted much attention on a visit to London. Notable too at that time was Madame Masson, the wife of the celebrated *paumier* of the rue Mazarine and St Honoré courts in Paris. She was credited with a supple wrist and a sturdy volley, but also with unacceptably quarrelsome behaviour on court.[6]

In England there is no record of any woman player before Baroness Wentworth, who built a court on her estate at Crabbet Park, Sussex in 1907 and published two sonnets on the game. As her professional she employed G. F. Covey, who was later to win the world championship and hold the title between 1912 and 1928. Under his tuition she was said to have developed form quite astonishing in a lady,[7] but cynics remarked more on the difficulty of beating her on her own court when Covey was marking.

The wives of professionals were naturally to the fore among the steadily growing number of gifted players when women took to the game in the latter part of the twentieth century. Prominent amongst them, as both player and administrator, has been Lesley Ronaldson, married to the World Champion.

At Oxford, as women's play, women's matches and women's championships burgeoned everywhere, the university's enlarged intake of female undergraduates was reflected on the tennis court as more and more were made aware of the unique attractions of the game and welcomed to Merton Street. A team, named the Penthouse Pets, was formed, and a landmark in the history of tennis was reached in 1992 when the first women's Varsity match was held (Oxford winning by five matches to nil).

A development of a different kind was also in progress. Throughout the 1980s plans were being prepared to rebuild all the existing premises of the club with the exception of the court itself. In May 1990, after prolonged negotiations, Merton College's governing body signified its 'approval in principle to the proposal that should the tenants of the Real Tennis Court produce plans and raise funds for the rebuilding of the changing rooms and professional shop then Merton would be agreeable to grant a lease of up to fifty years for the whole of the property including the main court; terms for rent reviews and repairs liabilities to be agreed.'[8]

Meanwhile another new constitution was drawn up and adopted. This redefined yet again OUTC's status as a university club and The Unicorn Club's as a separate entity, but on this occasion the primary objective was the establishment of a charitable trust, The Oxford University Tennis Foundation, to take advantage of grants and tax benefits.

These arrangements have cleared the way for the launch of an Appeal for funds to meet the cost of the most ambitious building project in the previous two centuries of tennis in Oxford. The planning of the work has been supervised by Brigadier Browne, a member of the club and former bursar of Oriel, who was responsible for the recent transformation of the Oriel court.

In addition to improved club facilities for members and visiting players, and office and workshop facilities for the professionals, the rebuilding will provide much-needed living accommodation for a resident professional. Under the agreement with the college it will also bring with it the fulfilment of another long-sought aspiration: the greater security of a long-term tenancy.

The Appeal, in aid of which this history has been written, is scheduled to mark the four-hundredth anniversary of tennis in Merton Street, where the game was first played on the present site in 1595. It is to be hoped that the celebration of a quatercentenary will be seen as no more than a staging post on the road towards further centuries of enjoyment of this ancient game by gown and town, young and old, in the most congenial and appropriate of settings.

Appendices

Putto at Play

Appendix A

Diagram intended to explain the Game of Tennis to those who are not players but who take an interest in the game as lookers on.

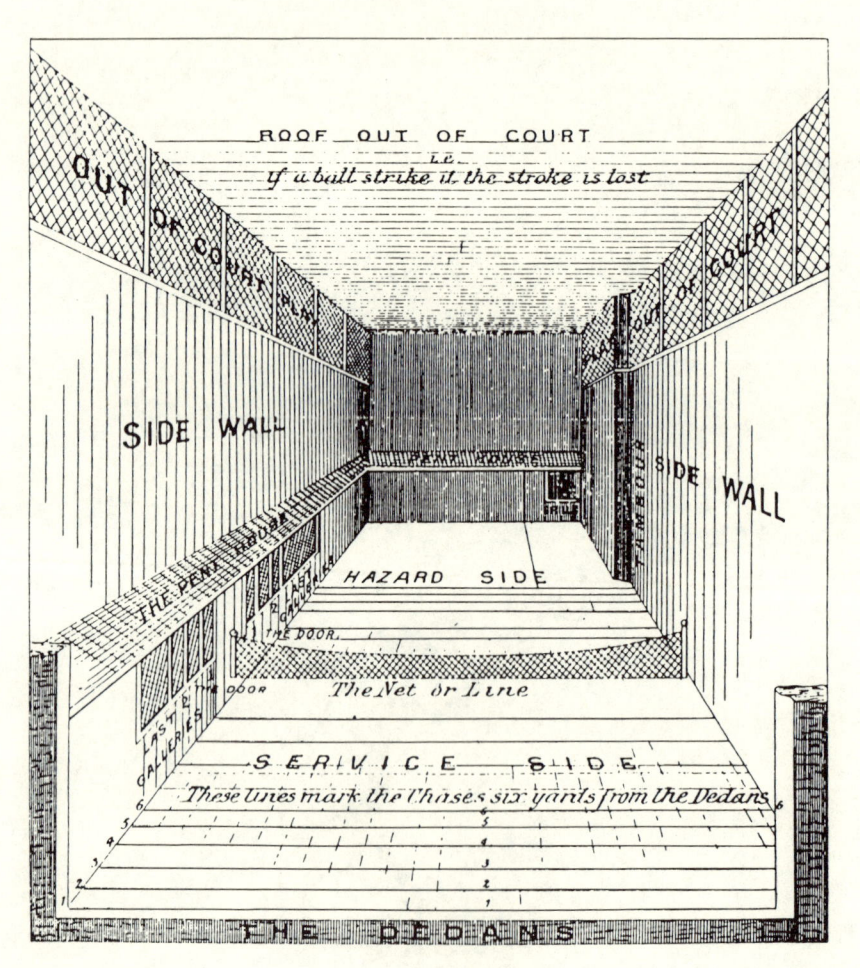

Internal View of a Court

APPENDIX A

Playing the Game[1]

The Court

A modern tennis court is a large rectangular building lit by a range of high side-windows, a glassed roof or artificial light. At the beginning of 1994 there were thirty-six such courts in active use throughout the world: nineteen in England, one in Scotland, three in France, nine in the USA and four in Australia. In addition, several openings and reopenings of new and disused courts were in the course of preparation, most importantly a project for a court in Washington, DC.

Some features of the courts, while similar, are not precisely uniform. The varying dimensions of the playing areas approximate to 96 feet in length and 32 feet in width at floor level. Oxford's court measures only 93 feet by 28½ and is the smallest.

A net divides each court into equal but dissimilar halves: the service side and the hazard side. Internal (battery) walls run round three sides of the court to a height of rather more than 7 feet (but in Oxford to just under 6½). These are surmounted by sloping roofs known as penthouses. All walls are in play (above, below and including the penthouses) up to a play-line which runs at a height of some 18 feet along the sides (under the windows) and 24 feet at the ends.

Beneath the end-wall penthouse on the service side is an opening in the internal wall some 3½ feet above floor level, measuring about 21½ feet in width and 3½ in height. This and the space behind it is the dedans, where spectators can sit on benches in a gallery or in a club room and watch the game through protective netting.

Similar openings and galleries run under the side-wall penthouse along most of one side of the court. In order from the service end these are: the last gallery, the second gallery, the door, the first gallery and, beyond the net (on the hazard side), hazard the first gallery, hazard the door, hazard the second gallery and the winning gallery. In a recess beside the net, between the two first galleries, stands the marker, whose job it is to call the score and the chases. The spaces either side of him in the marker's box are called the line and hazard the line. Here too is the entrance to the court, which is no longer by the two 'doors'. Nowadays these are doors in name only.

The end wall on the hazard side contains no galleries but instead, towards one corner, an opening an inch or two more than 3 feet square known as the grille. This is backed by a wooden panel, which is often decorated with an emblem or image such as a cardinal's hat, Henry VIII's head or the Oxford unicorn.

The fourth wall, facing the entrance to the court, is the main wall. It alone has a plain surface without openings, but this surface contains a special feature which is unique. An angled projection on the hazard side, called the tambour, narrows the court by some 18 inches for about 14 feet until it meets the end wall near the grille. The angle of the tambour, more or less acute, is one of the significant variations from court to court.

The dedans (on the service side) and the winning gallery and the grille (on the hazard side) are 'winning openings'. When a player strikes the ball into them from the opposite side of the net he gains the point.

The Chase

Penthouses, hazards and winning openings are distinctive features of tennis. The multitude of opportunities which they present bring to the game the fascination of its almost infinite variety. Yet at the heart of tennis lies a subtler peculiarity, derived from the earliest days of *longue paume*. This is the chase, which may be defined most simply as a point held in abeyance.

The floor on the service side of the court and on the half of the hazard side nearer the net is marked with chase lines. On the service side these mark the distance in yards from the end wall beneath the dedans. The figures 1 to 6 are painted on the side walls above the appropriate line, with half-yards indicated between. Beyond 6 yards, the lines mark the centre of each gallery, with an additional line one yard beyond the last gallery, and also with intermediate markings.

Gallery chase lines continue on the hazard side of the net, where they are followed by 2-yard and 1-yard lines indicating the distance, not from the end of the hazard side, but from a line bisecting this side of the court. The rear half of the hazard side is a winning area.

The scoring and basic method of play are those adopted for lawn tennis. Opponents strike the ball alternately from opposite sides of the net. If it passes over the net (or round it along or above the side penthouse) it has to be returned on the volley or after only one bounce on the floor. The number of walls struck by the ball is immaterial provided they are struck below the play-line; if above, or touching the roof, the ball is 'out of court'. Once it touches the floor a second time it is dead, but unless it falls within the winning area a chase has been laid and the point is neither won nor lost.

Thus in a rally (known, perversely, as a rest), if either player hits the ball into the net he loses the point, but should the player on the service side miss the ball completely the point is not yet decided. If the second bounce falls on the 3-yard line, for example, the marker will call 'chase three'. Then, when either player is within one point of game, or when a second chase is laid, the players will change ends and play off the chase.

The player from the service side will now be on the hazard side and, in the case of a 3-yard chase, must control each of his strokes to such a length that the second bounce will fall nearer to the end wall of the service side than the 3-yard line. If it falls further from the end wall, either on the floor or by entering a gallery, he loses the point. If it falls nearer or enters the dedans, he wins the point. If it falls on the 3-yard line itself, 'chase off' is called and the point is annulled.

Chases are laid also when the ball is hit into any of the side galleries, except the winning gallery. If it enters the second gallery on the service side, the call is 'chase the second gallery'. If it enters the second gallery on the hazard side, the call is 'hazard the second gallery'. In defeating a hazard chase the player on the hazard side has the whole of the service side and its galleries at his disposal.

Because service is always from the same side of the court and does not alternate with the games as in lawn tennis, a change of service occurs only when the players change sides, and this occurs only for the purpose of playing off chases. If no chase were laid by his opponent, the player who wins the toss and chooses to serve would continue serving throughout the match. Thus, whether the point is finally won or lost, a chase wins the right to serve. The receiver of service then becomes the server and holds service until dislodged by the laying of another chase.

For this reason the chase dictates the tactics of the game: 'To lay down a close chase is obviously what the player on the hazard side strives for and his opponent strives to prevent, for to lay a close chase has the double advantage, not only of going a long way towards winning a point, but also of gaining the service side, no small advantage in modern tennis.'[2]

Service

Service takes place along the side penthouse. The ball must touch the penthouse on the hazard side and strike the floor within the service court, which occupies the greater part of the rear half of the hazard side. For a service to be good it is immaterial whether or not the ball also touches the penthouse on the service side, the wall above the penthouse, the end penthouse on the hazard side, or the end wall.

This flexibility, enhanced by a rule which permits the server to serve from anywhere on his side of the court up to the second gallery line, accounts for the very large number of types and techniques of service, fluctuating greatly in pace and trajectory. These include such exotica as the bobble and the cherry-bob, the boomerang and the chandelle, the giraffe and the caterpillar, the pique and the demi-pique, but all fall into four general categories (with some hybrids): the side-wall, the drop, the railroad and the underhand twist. The deadliest of these is the fast, side-wall-hugging overhead railroad, formerly designated 'the American service' from its introduction into England by Tom Pettitt, the champion from Boston.[3]

The perfect service, fast or slow, makes a 'dead nick': that is, it falls from the penthouse to land in the junction of the floor with the end wall. Since the ball does then not rise it is impossible to return, so that the only possible response is to anticipate and volley the ball as it leaves the penthouse.

The powerful weapon of service is made even more so by the allowance of a second service when a fault is served. This dates from the time when the ball was put into play, not by one of the players, but by a servant who, if he failed to perform this service correctly, would be required to do it again. Play proper began with the return of service, which in the traditional nomenclature of tennis is *le premier coup*.

The survival of the second service into a century when serving has evolved into a match-winning stroke is an anachronism and an anomaly. It has upset the balance of advantage between players which the rules of all games should aim to preserve. Its effect on tennis has been notable but less marked than in some of its offshoots (in rackets, for example, and, most seriously, lawn tennis).

In returning service the receiver will usually attempt a chase, which (unless he is playing off a chase) will take him to the service side before the end of the game. The best of chases is 'better than half a yard', which can be beaten only by a shot into the dedans.

Alternatively, the receiver of service may try to win the point outright and aim for the dedans even when there is no short chase to beat. The dedans' wide expanse, yawning like a goal-mouth, presents a tempting target. It can be attacked effectively with a 'straight force' or a 'boasted force' off the main wall, and if the server succeeds in intercepting such a hard-hit ball he may mishit his return and lose the point by that means.

Stroke Play

To lay a short chase a player must master the technique of hitting the ball to a length. A stroke with this objective will necessitate either heavy undercutting or a stroking of the ball so that it will die in a corner.

For this reason the chase dictates not only tactics but the kind of stroke employed. This stroke is thus another peculiarity of tennis. It is played not so much from the wrist as in rackets and squash, nor from the shoulder as in lawn tennis, but more from the elbow. A full back swing is required, but little follow-through. The stroke is chopped off at the moment of impact in order to impart cut to a ball which, unlike a lawn tennis or squash ball, is solid and therefore much more receptive to spin.

The ideal return travels sufficiently fast for an opponent to be unable to prevent the ball reaching the end wall, but not so hard that it bounces back from the wall and can be played on the rebound. Hence the importance of undercutting, which brings the ball down sharply after contact with a wall.

Owing to the configuration of the court, the player on the service side is in much the stronger position, but he too is well advised to hit the ball to a length. This not only makes retrieval harder, but only the rear of the hazard side is a winning area and a short return or an over-hit one results in a hazard chase and loss of the service end. Alternatively, two of the three winning openings are available to him, one on each side of the court: the winning gallery and the grille. There is, too, the bonus of the tambour, a shot towards which may leave his opponent uncertain whether the ball will be deflected across the court by the angle of the wall or whether it will miss and pass on into the corner.

An important consideration for both players in stroke play is the sagging of the net by 2 feet from sides to middle. This permits a lower trajectory for cross-court and centre-court shots than for those directed along the side-walls. For this reason the former are the more effective.

In doubles, tactics and positioning are the key to success. It is normal for one player on the service side to defend the side galleries (to avoid losing the service end) and for one on the hazard side to guard the grille and tambour. Laying chases is as necessary as in singles but more difficult, and forcing opponents into error is often an easier option.

Handicapping

The bisque and cramped odds, the most entertaining methods of matching strong and weak players, are little used today.

The bisque is a wild card, like a joker. A player receiving one can take it at any time during the set except when the ball is in play. A call of 'bisque' is all that is needed to win the next point. But good judgement is needed too: to recognise the right moment to make use of it.

Cramped odds can be more finely tailored. 'Touch-no-walls', for example, means that a player so severely handicapped loses the point if a ball played by him touches a wall before its second bounce or enters any of the openings. A less restrictive variation, when players are more evenly matched, is 'bar the openings'.

The more usual system of handicapping is by points – 'fifteen', 'owe fifteen' and so on – which has become familiar in lawn tennis. A refinement in recent years has been the introduction of personal handicaps, as in golf. An even match between two players of differing ability is ensured by reference to a table showing the appropriate award or forfeiture of points according to the difference between their personal handicaps.

Tennis is thus a game which two or four players can enjoy together whatever their respective standards of play.

APPENDIX B
Oxford Blues and Half-Blues 1947–94

1947 G.P. Jackson
(Brasenose)
D.E. Mount
(Christ Church)

1948 G.P. Jackson
(Brasenose)
P.G.L. Curle
(Trinity)

1949 P.G.L. Curle
(Trinity)
M.M. Jones
(Trinity)

1950 I.P. Campbell
(Trinity)
M.M. Morton
(Brasenose)

1951 I.P. Campbell
(Trinity)
R.H.M. Kindersley
(Trinity)

1952 R.H.M. Kindersley
(Trinity)
A.H. Norton
(Corpus Christi)

1953 E.N.C. Oliver
(Exeter)
R.H. Searby
(Corpus Christi)

1954 R.H. Searby
(Corpus Christi)
J.T.C. Taylor
(Corpus Christi)

1955 M.R. Coulman
(Trinity)
R.B. Bloomfield
(Balliol)

1956 M.R. Coulman
(Trinity)
R.B. Bloomfield
(Balliol)

1957 R.B. Bloomfield
(Balliol)
S.A.M. Collins
(Magdalen)

1958 H.M.H. Glover
(Lincoln)
W.P.B. Gunnery
(Pembroke)

1959 J.E. Baily
(Corpus Christi)
The Hon. L.D. Verney
(New College)

1960 C.A.A. Black
(Christ Church)
C.J.D.L. Swallow
(New College)

1961	C.J.D.L. Swallow (New College) J.W. Leonard (Christ Church)		M.S. Travis (Trinity)
1962	J.R.N. Travis (Trinity) The Lord Dufferin and Ava (Christ Church)	1970	C.M. Wilmot (Corpus Christi) J.M. Potter (Jesus)
1963	J.R.N. Travis (Trinity) J.Q. Greenstock (Worcester)	1971	C.M. Wilmot (Corpus Christi) J.M. Potter (Jesus)
1964	U.D. Barnett (Magdalen) P.T.G. Philipps (Christ Church)	1972	C.J. Moore (Pembroke) D.P. Jessell (Balliol)
1965	P.T.G. Philipps (Christ Church) J.Q. Greenstock (Worcester)	1973	A.C. Lovell (Jesus) J.C.A. Leslie (Trinity)
1966	J.Q. Greenstock (Worcester) R.W.A. Bray (Corpus Christi)	1974	A.C. Lovell (Jesus) P.G. Seabrook (Oriel)
1967	R.W.A. Bray (Corpus Christi) P.P.M. Monbiot (Christ Church)	1975	A.C. Lovell (Jesus) P.G. Seabrook (Oriel)
1968	P.P.M. Monbiot (Christ Church) W.J.C. Surtees (Balliol)	1976	A.C. Lovell (Jesus) D.P. Jessell (Balliol) I.O. Goulty (Corpus Christi) R.F. Hollington (University)
1969	W.J.C. Surtees (Balliol)	1977	R.F. Hollington (University)

P.A. Luff
(St Catherine's)
W.A. Hollington
(St Edmund Hall)
F.C. Satow
(Trinity)
1978 M.F. Dean
(Keble)
W.A. Hollington
(St Edmund Hall)
F.C. Satow
(Trinity)
P.A. Luff
(St Catherine's)
1979 W.A. Hollington
(St Edmund Hall)
F.C. Satow
(Trinity)
P.A. Luff
(St Catherine's)
J.V. Hansford
(Christ Church)
1980 W.A. Hollington
(St Edmund Hall)
F.C. Satow
(Trinity)
J.D.S. Fricker
(Balliol)
A. Kanwar
(St Catherine's)
1981 W.A. Hollington
(St Edmund Hall)
J.D.S. Fricker
(Balliol)
P.J. McQuibban
(Wadham)

T.J. Taylor
(Magdalen)
1982 W.A. Hollington
(St Edmund Hall)
T.J. Taylor
(Magdalen)
C.I. Hardy
(St Edmund Hall)
N.C.J. Stutchbury
(Brasenose)
1983 R.G.P. Ellis
(St Edmund Hall)
A.J.C. Maxwell
(Worcester)
N.C.J. Stutchbury
(Brasenose)
R.N.H. Taylor
(Queen's)
1984 M.R.C. Swallow
(University)
A.J.C. Maxwell
(Worcester)
J.A. Betts
(Queen's)
W.R. Bristowe
(St Edmund Hall)
1985 J.A. Betts
(Queen's)
M.R.C. Swallow
(University)
J.M. Crocker
(Hertford)
P.R.V. Maxwell
(St Catherine's)
1986 J.A. Betts
(Queen's)

J.N. Jee
(Brasenose)
M.J. Harper
(Trinity)
P.R.Y. Maxwell
(St Catherine's)
1987 J.N. Jee
(Brasenose)
J.M. Crocker
(Hertford)
C.E.R.M. Hall
(Brasenose)
J.P. Lewis
(Christ Church)
1988 C.E.R.M. Hall
(Brasenose)
J.N. Jee
(Brasenose)
S.G. Harford
(St John's)
J.A. de Portales
(Merton)
1989 C.C. Parker
(Merton)
A.J.J. Thornton
(Wadham)
C. Cleaver
(Brasenose)
C.W. Birkle
(Hertford)
1990 A.M. Searle
(Worcester)
J.D. Emery
(Green)
P.S. Baldwin
(Merton)

R.A. Krznaric
(Pembroke)
1991 J.D. Emery
(Green)
R.A. Krznaric
(Pembroke)
A. Robinson
(Lady Margaret)
G.J. Baker
(Queen's)
1992 R.A. Krznaric
(Pembroke)
D.D.W. Reid
(Merton)
R.R. Montgomerie
(Worcester)
D.L. Finegold
(Pembroke)
1993 G.J. Baker
(Queen's)
R.R. Montgomerie
(Worcester)
A. Robinson
(Lady Margaret Hall)
G.R. Bowers
(Pembroke)
1994 R.R. Montgomerie
(Worcester)
R.D.M. Edwards
(Brasenose)
G.T. Rawstorne
(Jesus)
H.G.A. Birts
(Trinity)

Acknowledgments

In compiling this work I owe much to the assistance of a large number of books, manuscripts, institutions and individuals. Among the sources acknowledged in the following reference pages I have leaned most on those listed at the head of the section – by Julian Marshall, E. B. Noel & J. O. M. Clark, Lord Aberdare and Anthony Wood – together with the various volumes of Oxford records edited by the Reverend H. E. Salter and the printed and manuscript works of Percy Manning. Lord Aberdare has also most kindly read a draft and rescued me from some errors, and I am indebted too to Dr Roger Morgan of Cambridge, the historian of early tennis, for several amendments.

The services of the Bodleian Library and the County Council's Centre for Oxfordshire Studies have been indispensable, and I must record my gratitude also to Michael Mayhew of the Ashmolean Museum, Dr Lauren Gilmour of the Museum of Oxford and Oliver Everett, the Librarian of Windsor Castle. College archivists and librarians have been most helpful, and I am especially indebted to Mrs Elizabeth Boardman, the archivist of Oriel and Brasenose Colleges, Dr Mark Curthoys of Christ Church, Dr Steven Gunn and John Burglass of Merton, Mrs Naomi Van Loo of Pembroke and Mrs Caroline Dalton of New College.

The reminiscences of John Cook, Peter Dawes, Mick Dean, Peter Ellis, Michael Flanagan, Michael Maclagan, Michael Meyer and Chris Ronaldson have shed light on the recent past. Richard Vallat has helped with research, and records have been kindly made available by Brigadier Myrtle of the Tennis and Rackets Association and James Railton of the University of Oxford Committee for Sport. Illustrations have been expertly reproduced by Jerry Broad. Among overseas correspondents Dr Richard Travers, of Melbourne, has been of great assistance. Others who have elucidated particular points for me are acknowledged under the relevant references.

Acknowledgments

Lastly but above all, my thanks go to Dr Bruce Henning, the Senior Treasurer of OUTC, whose idea it was to mark the quatercentenary of the Merton Street courts by launching me on this voyage of exploration and discovery. I only hope that it proves as interesting to members of the club and the tennis fraternity generally – even to the uninitiated seeking enlightenment and to students of the byways of Oxford's history – as it has to me. Dr Henning's assistance with the illustrations, Appendix B and the index has also been invaluable.

The extract from the report on the future Edward VII by the prince's Governor is printed by the gracious permission of Her Majesty the Queen. The Visitor of Brasenose College's letters are reproduced by kind permission of the Principal and Fellows. The detail of the print of Pembroke College by Michael Burghers is reproduced by kind permission of the Master and Fellows. Details taken from David Loggan's views of the colleges are reproduced from a copy of *Oxonia Illustrata* in Worcester College library by kind permission of the Provost and Fellows. The illustration of the Prince of Wales receiving tuition on the Oriel Street court is reproduced from a print kindly loaned by David Cull of Lord's. Line drawings of putti are by Julian Bingley.

❖

Oxford University Tennis Club and The Unicorn Club gratefully acknowledge the generosity of Blackwell Scientific Publications, Oxford University Press and the Alden Press in producing this book without charge; also the assistance of Jonathan Conibear, William Alden and Edward Wates in its printing and publication. The clubs are also especially grateful to the author for assigning copyright and forgoing royalties. The Oxford University Tennis Foundation will be the beneficiary.

Source References

Abbreviations

Aberdare *for* Lord Aberdare, *The Willis Faber Book of Tennis & Rackets* 1980
Marshall *for* Julian Marshall, *The Annals of Tennis* 1878
Noel & Clark *for* E. B. Noel and J. O. M. Clark, *A History of Tennis* 1924
Salter *for* Rev. H. E. Salter
Wood, *City of Oxford* for Anthony Wood, *Survey of the Antiquities of the City of Oxford* ed. Andrew Clark 1889–99
Wood, *Life & Times* for *The Life and Times of Anthony Wood* ed. Andrew Clark 1891–1900

Chapter 1:
An Intellectual and Unlawful Pastime

1. J. M. Heathcote, 'Tennis' in The Badminton Library *Tennis, Lawn Tennis, Rackets, Fives* 1890, p. 106 (large paper ed. p. 114)
2. Ted Johnson, of Moreton Morrell, in conversation with the author
3. R. Lukin, *A Treatise on Tennis* 1822, p. 8
4. George Chapman, *The Tragedy of Charles Duke of Byron*, Act 3, scene i
5. J. K. Stephen, *Parker's Piece* 1891
6. 12 Ric. II cap. 6
7. 11 Hen. IV cap. 4
8. 17 Ed. IV cap. 3
9. 3 Hen. VIII cap. 3
10. N. E. McClure, *The Letters of John Chamberlain* 1939, Vol. I, p. 52
11. Stephen Penton, *The Guardian's Instruction* 1688, p. 53
12. 16 Ch. II cap.7

Source References

13 J. Earle, *Micro-cosmographie* ed. 1628, Chap. 24

Chapter 2: Origins and Growth

1 Donato Velluti, *Cronica di Firenze*, quoted in Noel & Clark, p. 567
2 *Fitzstephen's Description of the City of London* 1772, p. 74
3 Albert de Luze, *La Magnifique Histoire du Jeu de Paume*, Bordeaux 1933, pp. 28, 29
4 *Letters and Papers of John Shillingford* 1871, p. 101
5 Book IV, l. 460. For racket as a game of dice see *OED*.
6 Lines 295–8
7 Henry V, Act I, scene ii
8 *John Benet's Chronicle* in Camden Misc. Vol. XXIV 4th Series Vol. 9 1972, p. 218
9 *Poesies*, ed. P. V. Chalvet, Grenoble 1803, p. 347
10 Act V, scene iv
11 *The Countess of Pembrokes Arcadia* 1598, Lib. 5, p. 453
12 John Hewytt, *Nine Select Sermons*, 1658, p. 60
13 *Familiarium Colloquiorum*, Basle 1529, pp. 64, 65
14 *Leges Ludi* 1539 in Foster Watson, *Tudor School-boy Life* 1908, p. 203
15 Act III, scene ii
16 Richard Mulcaster, *Positions* (1581) 1888 ed., p. 105
17 Henry Peacham, *Minerva Britanna* 1612, p. 113
18 *Oxford English Dictionary*
19 *Description des arts et metiers par l'Academie royale des sciences*, Paris 1767

Chapter 3: The Golden Age

1 33 Hen. VIII cap. 9
2 2 & 3 Phil. & Mary cap. 9
3 Maistre Estienne Perlin, quoted in Marshall, p. 69
4 *Gul's Horne-booke* 1812, p. 24

5 *The Survey or Topical Description of France* 1592, pp. T4 verso and V
6 *The Works of Francis Rabelais MD*, tr. Urquart & Motteux, ed. J. Ozell 1750, Vol. II, p. 37
7 *An Essay Concerning Human Understanding* 1690, Chap. XXI, sec. 9
8 *Leges Ludi* 1539 in Foster Watson, *Tudor School-boy Life* 1908, p. 208
9 *The Nobles or of Nobilitye* 1563, Book 3
10 p. 263
11 pp. 3, 4
12 1880 ed., Vol. I, p. 292
13 p. 62
14 1888 ed., p. 105
15 *Renaissance Quarterly* Vol. XXXIV 1981, pp. 26, 27
16 *Trattato del Giuoco della Palla*, tr. W. W. Kershaw 1951, pp. x, xi
17 *Description des arts et metiers par l'Academie royale des sciences*, Paris 1767
18 *Basilicon Doron* 1603, pp. 120–1
19 Aberdare, p. 55
20 Wood, *Life & Times* Vol. I, p. 75
21 Aberdare, p. 55
22 Diary, 4 January 1664
23 Diary, 2 September 1667

Chapter 4: Early Days in Oxford

1 Salter, *Regulum Cancellarii Oxoniensis 1434–1469* Vol. I (OHS Vol. XCII) 1932, pp. 213–4
2 Snappe's Formulary (OHS Vol. LXXX) 1924, p. 233
3 Bodl. MS Twyne XXIII, f. 388; W. H. Turner, *Selections from the Records of the City of Oxford* 1880, p. 13
4 Salter, *Registrum Annalium Collegii Mertonensis 1483–1512* 1923, pp. x and 156
5 W. H. Turner, *Selections from the Records of the City of Oxford* 1880, p. 86

Source References

6 Salter, *Oxford City Properties* (OHS Vol. LXXXIII) 1926, p. 321
7 Wood, *Life & Times* Vol. II, p. 229
8 Bodl. MS (Manning) Top. Oxon d. 202, pp. 453, 454
9 *Ibid.* p. 455
10 Salter, *Oxford City Properties* (OHS Vol. LXXXIII) 1926, p. 323
11 *Ibid.* pp. 320-2
12 W. H. Turner, *Selections from the Records of the City of Oxford* 1880, p. 364
13 *Calendar of the Patent Rolls 1554-1555* 1936, p. 79
14 *Calendar of the Patent Rolls 1566-1569* 1964, p. 81

Chapter 5: College Ball Courts

1 Brasenose Vice-Principal's Register 1594-1710, pp. 24, 25
2 *Brasenose College, Oxford, Visitors' Injunctions, etc.* 1853, pp. 72, 73
3 W. P. Ellis, *Liber Albus Civitatis Oxoniensis* 1909, p. 117
4 For Cambridge courts see Willis & Clark, *The Architectural History of the University of Cambridge* 1886
5 *Ibid.* Vol. I, p. 574
6 Vol. IV, pp. 94, 95
7 Vivian H. H. Green, *The Commonwealth of Lincoln College 1427-1977* 1979, p. 218
8 Magdalen College *Liber Computi*
9 *Brasenose Quatercentenary Monographs* 1909, Vol. II, p. 19
10 I am indebted to the Trinity Archivist, Mrs Clare Hopkins, for this suggestion.
11 Wood, *City of Oxford* Vol. I, p. 358
12 *Victoria History of the County of Oxford* Vol. III, Ichnographia facing p. 92
13 Salter, *Oxford Balliol Deeds* (OHS Vol. LXIV) 1913, pp. 90 and 341
14 *Ibid.* p. 155
15 C. W. Boase, *Registrum Coll. Exon.* 1894, p. xciii
16 *Liber Implementorum Coll. Exon. 1618-38* (Dr Prideaux's Survey), Peryam's Mansions Cap. 4

17 Wood, *City of Oxford* Vol. I, p. 68
18 *Ibid.* pp. 535, 536
19 Herbert Hurst, *Oxford Topography* (OHS Vol. XXXIX) 1899, p. 148. See also Agas's Map 1578 and Agas's Map of Oxford with Bereblock's Views 1728, both in *Old Plans of Oxford* (OHS Vol. XXXVIII) 1884
20 David Watson Rannie, *Oriel College* 1900, p. 107
21 Richards & Salter, *The Dean's Register of Oriel 1446–1661* 1926, pp. 325-6
22 Council Book d. f. 362b, quoted in Douglas Macleane, *A History of Pembroke College, Oxford* 1897, pp. 276, 277
23 Anthony Wood, *The History and Antiquities of the Colleges and Halls in the University of Oxford* 1786, p. 150
24 W. C. Costin, *The History of St John's College, Oxford 1598–1860* 1958, p. 95
25 *Terrae-Filius* 1726, p. 184
26 *Ibid.*
27 Bursar's Private Account Book f. 33
28 Wood, *City of Oxford* Vol. I, p. 568
29 Issue dated 29 September 1793

Chapter 6: Courts, Inns and Theatres

1 3rd Edition, p. 11
2 Wood, *Life & Times* Vol. I, p. 53
3 Salter, *Surveys & Tokens* (OHS Vol. LXXV) 1920 [1923], p. 391
4 Wood, *Life & Times* Vol. II, p. 349
5 *Ibid.* Vol. I, p. 242
6 Salter, *Surveys & Tokens* (OHS Vol. LXXV) 1920 [1923], p. 394
7 *The Diary of Thomas Crosfield* ed. F. S. Boas 1935, p. 79
8 Wood, *Life & Times* Vol. II, p. 226
9 Bodl. MS Don. b. 12 (31)
10 Diary, 20 November 1660
11 Paul Ranger, 'Theatrical Ghosts' in *Oxford Times Limited Edition* November 1988, No. 25, pp. 12, 13

Source References

Chapter 7: The Blue Boar Courts

1. Christ Church MS *Book of Evidences* Part I, f. 170
2. Bodl. MS Twyne VI ff. 180, 210
3. Issue dated 21 June 1760
4. Issue dated 21 May 1763
5. Issue dated 13 April 1765
6. Christ Church MS Estates 144, ff. 164, 168
7. George Webbe Dasent, *Half a Life* 1874, p. 229

Chapter 8: The Oriel Street Courts

1. Salter, *Survey of Oxford* Vol. I (NS Vol. XIV) 1960, p. 184
2. *Oriel Record* 1963
3. *Oriel College Record* 1990 & 1992
4. Brian Durham and Ric Tyler, 'Oxford: Oriel College, Real Tennis Court' in *South Midlands Archaeology* CBA Group 9 Annual Newsletter 1993, p. 75
5. Wood, *Life & Times* Vol. I, p.75
6. Oriel College Deeds
7. *Jackson's Oxford Journal*, 27 August 1765
8. Museum of Oxford
9. For this estimate I am indebted to the urologists, Donald Urquart-Hay and Joseph Smith
10. 16 December 1769
11. 23 December 1769
12. Marshall, pp. 98 & 129
13. (and below). Shadwell & Salter, *Oriel College Records* 1926, pp. 212–215
14. (and below). Oriel College Deeds
15. *Ibid.*
16. Letter from Geoffrey Wagner in *Oxford Today* June 1990, p. 52

Chapter 9: The First Merton Street Court

1. Merton College Register of Leases 6.1, f. 44

2 6.1, f. 186b
3 Bodl. MS Wood Empt. 26, pp. 2, 3
4 Merton College Register of Leases 6.2, f. 3
5 Wood, *Life & Times* Vol. I, p.69
6 Merton College Register of Leases 6.2, f. 622
7 *Ibid.* 6.3, f. 34
8 Wood, Life & Times Vol. I, p. 77
9 *Ibid.* Vol. II, p. 217
10 *Ibid.* Vol. II, p. 270
11 Merton College Register of Leases 6.5, f. 218; 6.6, f. 61; 6.6, f. 374
12 *Ibid.* 6.7, f. 172
13 *Ibid.* 6.8, f. 101

Chapter 10: A Dynasty of Champions

1 Marshall, p. 102
2 *Jackson's Oxford Journal*, 4 May 1763
3 *Ibid.* 20 July 1757
4 *Ibid.* 14 May 1763
5 *Ibid.* 25 February 1768
6 Marshall, p. 103
7 *Ibid*, p. 106
8 J. M. Heathcote, 'Tennis' in The Badminton Library *Tennis, Lawn Tennis, Rackets, Fives* 1890, p. 113 (large paper ed. p. 122)
9 Aberdare, p. 82

Chapter 11: The Nineteenth-Century Renaissance

1 British Library Add. MSS 59415
2 *Annals of My Early Life 1806–1846* 1891, pp. 60, 61
3 *Half a Life* 1874, pp. 229–31
4 Royal Archives, Windsor Castle
5 Copy in Christ Church archives
6 Recollections of Dean Fremantle 1921, p. 41
7 Merton College Register of Leases 1836–1849, f. 199
8 Merton College Register of Leases 1861–1868, f. 7

Source References

9. *Ibid.* f. 23
10. *Ibid.* f. 142
11. *Ibid.* f. 302
12. Noel & Clark, p. 76
13. For this extract and other information about Smith Travers from his family's archives, I am indebted to Dr Richard Travers of Melbourne
14. For information about Thomas Stone I am indebted to his great-grandson, John Stanley-Rogers
15. For this information I am indebted to two Bostonians: Richard L. Brickley, Jr. and Hunnewell's grandson, also named Hollis Hunnewell
16. Malcolm D. Whitman, *Tennis Origins and Mysteries* New York 1932, pp. 55–58
17. Noel & Clark, p. 248

Chapter 12: Modern Times in Oxford

1. *Racquets, Tennis, and Squash* 1902, p. 186
2. M. R. Ridley, 'Tennis' in *Oxford* Vol. I, no. 2, 1934
3. OUTC Committee Minutes dated 30 October 1967
4. *The Times*, 17 March 1978
5. Marshall, p. 5
6. *Ibid*, p. 42
7. Noel & Clark, p. 57
8. Letter dated 17 May 1990 in OUTC Committee Minute Book

Appendix A: Playing the Game

1. This Appendix is based on an article by the author in *The Oxford Companion to Sports & Games* (OUP) 1975
2. Noel & Clark, p. 414
3. See Chris Ronaldson, *Tennis: A Cut above the Rest* 1985, Chap. 11

Index

*'Plate' refers to illustrations between pages 56 and 57
and pages 104 and 105*

Aberdare, Lord viii, 107, 108, 110, Plate
Agas 42, 46
Agas Hall 67
Agincourt 12
Aiken, S. Carolina 104
Alfred Street 36
All Souls College 40, 42
Amhurst, Nicholas 53
Andrewes, Richard 29
Angus, Howard 111, 114
apprenticeship 59, 72, 98, 99
Arcadia 13
archery 3, 22, 23
Ascham, Roger 23
Ashmolean Museum 58, 59
Aubrey, John 21
Australia 99, 101, 102, 104, 114, Plate

badminton 42, 111
Baerlein, Edgar 97
Baker, Gordon 118
Ballarat 101, 117
Balliol College 40, 43, 45, 92, 95, 96, 109
Baring, Mark 110
Baring, Maurice 109
Barlowe, William, Bishop of Lincoln 33, 34, Plates
Barre, Edmond 84, 85, 100
battoir 13, 35
Bear Lane 63
Bedford, Duke of 89
Beek, Professor J. 28
Benbowe, Robert 63
Betterton, Thomas 60
Biboche 85
Bishop Robinson 47
bishops of Lincoln 28, 30, 33, 34, Plates
bisque 8, 130
Blake, Thomas 28
Blois 12

Blue Boar Lane 56, 57, 58, 60, 61, 62, 63, 64, 65, 68, 70, 82, 91, 112
Blues, Oxford 107, Appendix B
Bodleian Library 100
Boston, Mass. 102, 103
Bostwick, James 105
Bostwick, Peter 105
bowls 3, 6, 36, 38, 39, 41, 42, 43, 48
boxing 60, 91
Brasenose College 33, 34, 35, 36, 40, 41, 42, 43, 115, Plates
Brasenose Lane 45
Brighton 75, 84, 87, 90
Broadgates Hall 78
Brougham Hall 90
Browne, Brigadier Hugh 120
Bruce, Colonel 92
Bruce, Hon. C.N. *see* Aberdare, Lord
Bruce, Hon. M.G.L. *see* Aberdare, Lord
Bull Inn 61
Bunel, Mlle. 83, 119
Burghers, Michael 48, 51
Burnham, Joane 57
Burnham, Thomas 56, 57, 58, 59, 60, 61, 64, 68, 79
Bushy, Henry 29
Bust, William 64
Butler, Thomas 59, 68

Cadogan, Earl of 93, 94
caitche 9, 25
caitchspeel 9
Cambridge 1, 2, 37, 38, 39, 54, 90, 94, 96, 104, 107, 114, 115, 117, 118
Campden, 3rd Viscount 5
Canford 90
Cardinal College 63
Carfax Conduit 64, 82
Carravagio 4
Cass, William 108, 109
Castiglione 23

147

Index

Castile, King of 14, 15
Cat Hall 54
Catherine the Great 65
Cazalet, P.V.F. 107
Cazalet, V.A. 107
Chancellor (of University) 28, 91
Charles I 5, 25, 27, 59, 68, 92
Charles II 27
Charles V (of France) 4
Charles IX (of France) 25
chase 9, 11, 12, 37, 67, 68, 126–8
Chaucer, Geoffrey 10
chess 1, 10
Chicago 61, 103
Christ Church 21, 40, 44, 45, 47, 53, 63, 64, 65, 68, 77, 91, 92, 95, 96
Christopher Hall 46
Church, Brian 117
Civil Wars 4, 25, 56, 68, 79
Clare College (Cambridge) 96, 117
Clarke, Somers 75
Clements, Henry 31
Clowe, Michael 29
Cobb, Francis 80
Coghan, Thomas 22
Condé, Prince de 119
Cook, John 118
Coombe Abbey 90
Cornmarket 100
Corpus Christi College 22, 40, 46, 78
Corpus Christi College (Cambridge) 37, 55
Il Cortegiane 23
courte paume 8, 11, 55
Covey, G.F. 119
Cox, George 85
Cox, Philip 84, 89
Cox, W.J. 84, 85
Crabbet Park 119
cramped odds 72, 73, 130
Crawley, C.S. 107
cricket 55, 94, 95, 107
Cromwell, Oliver 40
Crosfield, Thomas 60
Crown tavern 58
Cumnor 80

Dallington, Sir Robert 19
dancing 39, 60
Dasent, George Webbe 65, 66, 91, 92

Davies, Wayne 104
Dawes, Peter 110, 111, 113, 114, 115
Dean, Mick 116
dedans 8, 38, 90, 95, 125, 126, 127, 129
Dekker, Thomas 19
Denison, Henry 91
dicing 5, 10, 29
Dickinson, John 87, 108
Dickinson, Reginald 87
Divinity School 45
Dorset, Marquis of 14
Dragon School 110
draughts 10
Dublin 4, 61
Duchess of Malfi 13
Durham College 43

Eadle, Mark 117
Earle, John 7
East Sheen 89
Easton Neston 90
Edward III 3
Edward IV 4
Edward VII 74, 92, 93, Plate
Edwards, Katherine 68
Edwards, Richard 25, 59, 64, 68
Elizabeth I 5, 25
Ellis, Anne 80
Ellis, Mary 80
Ellis, Peter 110
Elyot, Sir Thomas 23
Embling, John 97
Emmanuel College (Cambridge) 38, 115
Erasmus 15, 16, 22, 35
Essex, Earl of 4, 25
Etchebaster, Pierre 104
Eton 95, 96
Exeter 10
Exeter College 40, 45, 46

Fairberd, William 40
Fairfax, General 41
Falkland Palace 38, 108
Ferrara, Duke of 24
Fife, Duke of 89
Fish Street 63
Fisher, John 97
Fitzstephen, William 9

Index

fives 13, 16, 37, 78, 94, 108, 109, 117
Flanagan, Michael 116
Florence 9
Folly Bridge 63, 70
football 3, 5, 9, 117
Forest Hill 82
Forrester family 103
Foulkes 73
Francis I (of France) 4
Frederick, Prince of Wales 74
Fremantle, Dean 94
Frewen Hall 92
Frogley, Richard 31

Galen 22, 23
Geneva 89
George III 70
George IV 70
Gibbon's court 61
giuoco della palla 9
Gloucester College 54
Gloucester Hall 54
Goethe 21
Goldsmith, Oliver 61
Goodhart, Arthur 109, 110
Goodwood 89, 106
Gould, Jay 105
Gower, John 2, 11
Graham, Reginald 110, 111
Gray, Edward 108
Gregory, Francis Nash 68, 75
Gregory, Mary 68, 75
Grenville, Lord 91
Gretton, Vice-Admiral Sir Peter 112
Grey, Earl, of Falloden 96
grille 8, 38, 54, 112, 126, 130
Groom, Jack 110
Grove Lane 47

Hainault, Margot of 119
Hall, Edward 5
Hampton Court 4, 90, 98, 99, 100, 103, 108, 114
The Hand and Racket 90
Hardaway family 72, 73, 75
Hardwick 80, 90
Harrow 95
Hart Hall 40, 53, 54
Hatfield House 90, 98, 106

The Haven of Health 22
Hayling Island 90, 113
Hemsley, John 64
Henning, Bruce 118
Henry II (of France) 24
Henry IV 3, 28
Henry IV (of France) 25
Henry V 12
Henry v 12
Henry VII 4
Henry VIII 3, 4, 5, 18
Henry, Prince of Wales 4, 25
Hertford College 31
Hewell Grange 90
Heythrop 61, 90
High Street 56, 58, 67, 68, 73
Hobart 100, 101
Hobbes, Thomas 21
Holt, Richard 29, 30, 53
Holyport 90, 106, 114
Hore, Agnes and John 43
Hudson 31, 59
Humberstone Abbey 10
Humfrey, Laurence 22
Hunnewell, Hollis Horatio 102
Hunt, Edward 98, 99, 102, 103, 104

Iffley Road 117
Iffley Mill 83
Irwin 92

Jackson's Oxford Journal 70
James I 25, 78
James II 26, 27
James Street court 83, 85, 87, 90, 95, 99, 100, 101
Jardine, D.R. 107
Jenkins, Richard 91
Jesmond Dene 90
Jesus College 40, 45, 46
Johns, Henry 110
Johnson family 103
Johnstone, Sir Frederick 93, 94
Jones, Micky 110

Keble College 116
Kettell, Ralph 43
King Edward Street 67, 76

Index

King's College (Cambridge) 38
Kinnoull, Earl of 110
Knox, Northrup 105
Krznaric, Roman 119
Kybald Lane 109
Kymer, Gilbert 28

Lakewood, N.J. 103, 104
Lambert, George 87, 98, 99, 102, Plate
Lambert, Thomas 99
Lant, Bartholomew 32, 63, 64
Lant, John 32, 63, 64, 77, 78
Laudian statutes 33
lawn tennis 11, 16, 55, 113, 116, 117, 129
Laws of Tennis 98
Lay, R.J. 110
Leamington 85, 90
Lees, Lowther 110
Leges Ludi 22
Leslie, John 116
Lincoln, bishops of 28, 30, 33, 34, Plates
Lincoln College 40, 54
Lincoln's Inn Fields 61
Little Gate court 31
Lloyd, Richard 70
Locke, John 21
Loggan, David 38, 39, 41, 42, 43, 44, 45, 46, 47, 48, 49, 50, 52, 54, 65, 77
London 9, 25, 27, 60, 80, 83, 85, 90, 95, 100, 110, 119
longue paume 8, 19, 41, 43, 55, 126
Lord's 84, 90, 95, 99, 110, 116
Louis XIV (of France) 27
Lovell, A.C. 107, 116
Ludekens, Kees 117, 118, Plate
Lyttelton, Hon. Alfred 97

Mabbott family 72, 75
Maclagan, Michael 110, 115
Macpherson, W.D. 110
Magdalen College 7, 36, 40, 41, 42, 95, 96
Magdalen College School 24, 112, 117
Magdalen Hall 21, 65, 91
Major, John 76
Manchester 87, 88, 89
Manhasset 104

Margot of Hainault 119
Marshall, Julian 86
Masson, Madame 119
rue Mazarine court 119
MCC Gold Racquet 107
Melbourne 101, 114
Melville, Hon. Ian Leslie 108
Merton College 7, 29, 40, 42, 46, 47, 53, 57, 77, 80, 95, 97, 108, 109, 118, 120
Merton Street 32, 39, 56–59, 61, 63, 68, 73–75, 77, 79, 82–85, 87, 90–92, 94, 97–99, 102, 108–113, 116, 117, 120, 121
Mews, P. 60
Miles, Eustace 97, 106
Mills 94
Milward, Alice 67
Molière 60
Montgomerie, Richard 119, Plate
More, Sir Thomas 21
Moreton Morrell 90, 106
Morrell, Frederick 97, 98
Much Ado About Nothing 15
Mulcaster, Richard 23
Museum of Oxford 42
Mylwarde, Henry 32, 67

Napoleon 89
New College 36, 40, 42, 46, 48, 95, 96
New College Lane 31, 46
New York 88, 102, 103, 104
Newport, Rhode Island 103

Oliver, Alan 116, 117
Orange Street 90
Oratory School 117
Oriel College 22, 40, 47, 49, 53, 67, 75, 76, 95, 118, 120
Oriel Street 25, 32, 56, 57, 58, 65, 67, 72, 74, 75, 76, 77, 79, 81, 84, 91, 92, 94, 96, 118, 120, Plates
Orléans 21
Orléans, Charles d' 12
Oseney Abbey 10
Otterbourne, Thomas 12
Oxford Seniors 112, 118
Oxford Unicorns 112
Oxford United Football Club 117

Index

Oxford University Tennis Club viii, 17, 108, 109, 110, 111, 112, 115, 120
Oxford University Tennis Foundation 120

Paris 5, 10, 15, 19, 20, 61, 84, 119
Parry, E. 68, 69, 70
Pembroke College 40, 47, 50, 51, 78, 119
Pembroke College (Cambridge) 38, 55, 96
Pembroke, Earl of 85
Penthouse Pets 120
Pepys, Samuel 27, 61, 70
Pettitt, Tom 102, 103, 104, Plate
Petworth 90, 106
Philadelphia 88, 103
Philips, William 29
Pillet, David 65, 70
Pillet, Susanna 65
Pillet, Thomas 65, 70, 71, 72
Postmasters Hall 77, 78, 79, 80
Prague 61
Prince Rupert 25, 68
Prince's Club 87, 90
Privy Council 30, 31
proctors 111

Queen's Club 90, 110
The Queen's College 40, 48, 53, 60

Rabelais 19, 21
The Racket Inn 63, 64
rackets 16, 37, 92, 94, 116, 117, 129
Radley College 110, 116
Rewley Abbey 10
Richard II 3, 28
Richmond and Gordon, Duke of 89
Ridley, Rev. Maurice 108, 109
Riseley, R.C. 107
Rome 4, 8
Ronaldson, Chris 112–117, 119, Plate
Ronaldson, Lesley 119
Ronaldson, Steve 116
Rousseau 21
Royal Academy of Sciences (France) 24
Royal Melbourne Tennis Club see Melbourne

Royal Tennis Court see Hampton Court
Russell, James 72, 73, 74, 84, 91, 92, 94, Plates
Russell, Jane 74

Sabin, Thomas 74, 84, 87, 95, 97, 98, 99
Sabin, William 97
St Aldate's 57, 61, 63
St Catherine's College 118
St Germain-en-Laye 27
St Honoré 119
St John's College 40, 48, 53, 118
St John's College (Cambridge) 38, 55
St Mary Hall Lane 67, 68, 69, 71
St Mary Magdalen 43
St Mary the Virgin 67
St Peter-in-the-East 46, 59
St Peter's College 116
St Petersburg 61, 65, 89
St Thomas, Chantry of 67
Salisbury, Marquess of 98
Salutation tavern 58
Sandwich 12
Scaino, Antonio 24
Scotland 4, 9, 25, 38, 90, 114
Seabrook, Peter 116
Seacourt Club 90, 113
Senior Unicorns Club 115
service 1, 81, 85, 128–9
Shakespeare, William 2, 11, 73
Ship Street 45
Sides, Henry 100
Sidney, Sir Philip 13
Singleton, John 40
skittles 3
Smith Gate courts 29–32, 45, 46, 54, 56, 59, 63
Southampton, Earl of 5
Sporting Magazine 55
squash 37, 116, 117
Stratfield Saye 88, 89, 106
Stone, Thomas 98–101, 114, Plate
Stone, Woolner 114
Stow, John 9
Summertown 74
Sun Court, Troon 114
Swedenborg 21

Index

tambour 8, 9, 54, 76, 81, 126, 130
Tennis and Rackets Association viii, 17, 107, 108, 112
Thayer, Nathaniel 102
Theatre Royal, Oriel Street 73
Theatre Royal, Windsor 61
Theobald's 90
Thornton, Edward 40
Thornton, Henry 61
The Times 55, 110, 116, Plate
Toldervey, Henry 31
Tompkins, Alfred 87, 88, 98
Tompkins, Edmund (1st) 82, 83
Tompkins, Edmund (2nd) 83
Tompkins, Edmund (3rd) aka Peter 83, 84, 85, 87
Tompkins, Edmund (4th) 75, 85, 86, 87, 89, 90, 98, 99, 100, 108, Plate
Tompkins, Frederick 88
Tompkins, George 82
Tompkins, John, 84, 87, 98
tradesmen's tokens 58, 59, Plate
Travers, Samuel Smith 99, 100
Trinity College 40, 43, 110, 116
Trinity College (Cambridge) 55, 96, 117
Troilus and Criseyede 10
Troon 114
Tudor, Queen Mary 18
Turin 89
Tuxedo Country Club 104

Unicorn Club viii, 112, 120
Unicorn Inn 57, 64
Unicorn Rackett Court 57
United States of America 99, 102, 103, 104
University College 40, 52, 53, 78, 95, 96, 109, 112
Upper Heyford 75, 98
Utopia 21

Valencia 15

Varsity matches 94, 95, 96, 106, 116, 118, 120
Vawse, John 63
Versailles 55
Vice-Chancellor 30, 60, 73, 91
Victoria, Queen 92
Vienna 89
Vinehall Lane court 36
Vives, Juan Luis 15, 22

Wadham College 40, 42, 43, 70
Wadlow, Charles 98
Warlman, John 29
Waryn, John 28
Waterperry 82, 88
Webb, William 87
Webster, John 13
Wellington court 96
Wellington, Duke of 88, 89
Wentworth, Baroness 119
White family 103
Whitehall 25, 27
Whitney courts 103, 104
Whyte, William 28
Williams, William 36, 48
Wilson, Duncan 108
Wimbledon Lawn Tennis Museum 107
Winchester 96, 116
Windmill Street court 83
Windsor Castle 14, 15
Wither, George 7
Woburn 89, 106
Wood, Anthony 25, 31, 39, 45, 46, 48, 54, 56, 57, 59, 68, 78, 79, 80
Wood family 57, 79, 80
Wood, Thomas (father of Anthony) 59, 77, 78, 79
Wood, Thomas 31, 59
Wood, Thomas (also Woods) 58, 59, 68
Worcester College 54, 119
Wordsworth, Charles 91
Wroth, Professor Peter 115